D1204784

It's Always *the Heart*

Arthur E. Constantine, MD

WESTBOW·
PRESS
A DIVISION OF THOMAS NELSON
& ZONDERVAN

WestBow Press books may be ordered through booksellers or by contacting:

WestBow Press
A Division of Thomas Nelson & Zondervan
1663 Liberty Drive
Bloomington, IN 47403
www.westbowpress.com
1 (866) 928-1240

Because of the dynamic nature of the Internet, any web addresses or links contained in this book may have changed since publication and may no longer be valid. The views expressed in this work are solely those of the author and do not necessarily reflect the views of the publisher, and the publisher hereby disclaims any responsibility for them.

Any people depicted in stock imagery provided by Thinkstock are models, and such images are being used for illustrative purposes only. Certain stock imagery © Thinkstock.

ISBN: 978-1-4908-2941-8 (sc)
ISBN: 978-1-4908-2942-5 (hc)
ISBN: 978-1-4908-2940-1 (e)

Library of Congress Control Number: 2014904470

Printed in the United States of America.

WestBow Press rev. date: 5/19/2014

Scripture taken from the Holy Bible, NEW INTERNATIONAL VERSION®. Copyright © 1973, 1978, 1984 by Biblica, Inc unless otherwise noted. All rights reserved worldwide. Used by permission. NEW INTERNATIONAL VERSION® and NIV® are registered trademarks of Biblica, Inc. Use of either trademark for the offering of goods or services requires the prior written consent of Biblica US, Inc.

Contents

Prologue

Our Inseparable Physical and Spiritual Hearts

As I made my way through medical school, internal medicine residency, cardiology fellowship, and private practice, I can remember a time when I did not realize the amazing, inseparable intertwining of the physical and spiritual hearts. This revelation was a process that began with looking at the concordance of a tabbed Bible and reading what God says about the heart. As a cardiologist with many years devoted to becoming an expert at understanding, diagnosing, and treating the complexities of the physical heart, it made sense that my fellowship with God would be deepened by reading and studying what He says about the heart. After all, the heart must be of paramount importance to God— He references the heart over seven hundred times in the Bible, more than all other organs combined ... more than the biblical mentions of life, belief, joy, knowledge, and believe it or not, even salvation. More importantly, I could not consider my training complete until I had a full understanding of the importance of the heart to God.

The importance of the physical heart to our lives is obvious to all. The heart beats over 100,000 times a day, seven days a week, 365 days a year—which equals over 36 million times a year (hopefully for ninety-plus years of life on earth)! The heart never stops working. Even while we sleep and rejuvenate our minds and bodies, the heart continues its rhythmic job of efficiently pumping blood and oxygen to all of our organs, supplying them with everything they need to stay alive. Without the heart, we cannot live precious seconds. We can live without any other organ, yet not without the heart. Even in a coma and with no visible brain function, we are still alive until the heart stops. Other diseases may ravage our bodies; however, we continue to live until the heart is overwhelmed and stops beating.

It takes work to maintain a physical heart in top condition. For the most part, our health is a direct result of the choices we make. Maintaining optimal heart health requires the commitment of time and effort to daily exercise, healthy food choices, and avoidance of substances unhealthy for our bodies. Simply put, we must be good stewards of the gift of health God freely gave to us. Once God revealed the importance of the spiritual heart to me, it was easy to see the undeniable parallel importance of the physical heart to life here on earth and the spiritual heart to life here and life everlasting in heaven. Just as the heart is the most important organ in our physical bodies for life on earth, it is the most important organ in our spiritual lives and life everlasting in heaven. The similarities of the physical and spiritual hearts are striking, and I am certain this is not by coincidence!

God is the God of hearts and wants our hearts. God desires that we know and trust Him so much that we give Him our hearts. In the Bible, God says, "I will give them a heart to know me, that I am the LORD. They will be my people, and I will be their God, for they will return to me with all their heart" (Jeremiah 24:7).

He communicates to us through our hearts. A strong spiritual heart must be soft and receptive to God's Word. Without a strong spiritual heart that accepts Jesus Christ as Lord, we cannot have life everlasting in heaven. No other organ can replace the heart's importance in eternal life. Just as it requires the commitment of time and effort to preserve the health of our physical hearts, the same commitment of time and effort to study God's Word is required for a spiritual heart to stay strong through the trials of this life that we will assuredly face. Through the grace of Jesus Christ, our spiritual hearts continue to supply us with what we need to live life to its fullest here on earth and for eternity in heaven.

Without the study of God's Word, it will be difficult to know what He says about us and wants for our lives. We become deceivable, making it hard to begin and maintain lasting change for a healthy life. To get the harvest of a long and healthy life, we must arm ourselves with His instructions to overcome the distractions preventing us from receiving this bounty.

It is impossible to separate the intertwining of the physical and spiritual hearts. God's revelation has led me to develop the truth that *it's always the heart,* which helps me better treat (and witness to) the patients He has put in my life. I am now better able to effect lasting change as I share the heart-changing message that it's always the heart.

The patient stories in this book are a general representation of a life's work as a cardiologist. The patients are chosen to reflect the most common issues of the heart that I have encountered over the years. The stories are about no specific patient(s), and any similarity in name is purely coincidental and sometimes chosen to illustrate a point. It is my hope that readers see themselves in many or all of the chapters, as the message of it's always the heart is for everyone.

Each patient story hopefully provides meaningful insights into how we can change our hearts so we can receive the physical and spiritual hearts and life God wants us to have! Most importantly, if you put these insights into action in your life, you will get results immediately that will last a lifetime.

Chapter 1

A Haughty Heart

Before a downfall the heart is haughty, but humility comes
before honor.

—Proverbs 18:12 TNIV

As is quite typical of my daily routine, I was running well behind in my
schedule when I picked up the chart of a new patient and walked into
the exam room. I quickly discovered, however, that this was going to be
anything but a typical exam. I was caught off guard—not by his physical
condition, but by the level of frustration written all over his face. If looks
could kill, I would have been already standing in line at the pearly gates.

"I have had time to take a nap waiting on you to come in here," he
snapped, anxiously glancing at the face of his Rolex.

Clearly here was a man of significant importance—or self-
importance—impeccably dressed in a pinstriped suit, starched shirt,
and power tie. Yet honestly, I considered him no more or less important
than any of the patients I would see throughout the day.

"Sorry I've gotten you off schedule," I responded while scanning
his chart.

I know by firsthand experience the unavoidable delays when seeing a
doctor. Despite being "one of the boys," I too experience long wait times
if my doctor is attending to the needs of patients who've signed in ahead
of me. I always acknowledge my regrets to patients for necessary delays,
but "Mr. Important," as I'll call him, did not accept my apology. I was

clearly keeping Mr. Important from something important, but really, what could be more important than his heart? Ironically, Mr. Important was busy dictating instructions to underlings in his organization on his cell phone while he waited on me. I asked myself, *Is Mr. Important's anger disguising the real reason he is seeing me today, or perhaps, is his anger the reason he is in my exam room?*

I understood Mr. Important's predicament. I could even understand his primary concern. Like Mr. Important, who among us hasn't felt as though he or she didn't have time to be sick? On the one hand, he was annoyed that the chest discomfort he had experienced over the last six weeks had worsened, yet oddly, on the other hand, he was much more annoyed that his wife had forced him to interrupt his very busy schedule to see a doctor.

In response to my questions about the origin of his chest pains, he briefly explained that his chest discomfort had begun six weeks earlier while he was rushing to catch an airline flight for a *very important* overseas business meeting in France. In a rather obvious effort to control the dialog of the examination, Mr. Important repeatedly corrected me, emphasizing that he was experiencing chest *pressure*, not chest *pain*. No doubt he, like many patients, was trying to convince me that pressure was not as severe as pain and therefore convince me it was not his heart. However, more than twenty-five years of practicing cardiology had taught me that especially in the case of personalities like Mr. Important, *it's always the heart.*

So here we had nearly sixty-year-old Mr. Important rushing through the airport, pulling an overstuffed rolling suitcase in one hand, while clutching a carry-on bag and briefcase with the other.

"At first," he said, "I chalked it up to the spicy lunch I had prior to heading to the airport. So when I finally got seated on the plane, I grabbed some Tums out of my briefcase, but the pressure didn't completely go away."

He explained he felt discomfort during his entire four-day stay in Paris, and the pressure feeling became more frequent with each day. By the final day of his trip, even walking a few steps to the bathroom would cause similar pressure, yet it would go away within five minutes of lying on one of the sofas in his suite.

At first Mr. Important denied that his discomfort would begin while resting. However, as I began to probe a little further with questions, he reluctantly admitted he "may have had a few mild episodes" at home when resting—one of which awakened him from a sound sleep and was accompanied by an alarming shortness of breath.

"I took my routine remedy of Tums and aspirin," he concluded, "and the pain went away after I walked out on the front porch for a few minutes."

This was an unexpected moment with Mr. Important because it was the first time since entering the exam room that he had become honest with me (and himself) by coming to grips with the seriousness of the situation and referring to his discomfort as pain. At the time, neither of us knew there would be more of these unexpected moments during the course of my treatment of him.

God warns us about the destructive nature of a haughty heart throughout the Bible. For example, in Psalm 101:5, He tells us, "... whoever has haughty eyes and a proud heart, him will I not endure." Later, Proverbs 16:5 says, "The Lord detests all the proud of heart. Be sure of this: They will not go unpunished."

Webster's Dictionary defines haughty as "from the root haught, which means high, having or assuring great pride in oneself and contempt for others; arrogance." It is precisely this prideful arrogance against which God strongly warns us.

In the case of Mr. Important, it appeared God was magnifying the warning. Yet as obvious as it seemed to everyone else in his life—particularly his wife—Mr. Important felt that any disease, especially heart disease, was beneath him. After all, he was in *full control* of every aspect of his life. He was a well-respected business leader. He wanted nothing. He needed nothing. He had no family history of premature heart disease. He had quit his pack-and-a-half-per-day cigarette habit cold turkey over eight years earlier (insinuating the weakness of others who, unlike him, had no control over their bad habits).

However, the things Mr. Important deemed hard in his life seemed to trouble him most. He was angry because his business life of important travel, meetings, and dinners robbed him of quality time with his wife, son, daughter and friends. He was proud—perhaps too proud—of the fact that his determination to succeed was born from an impecunious beginning. Coming from a poor family, where he shared bedrooms and even beds with his brothers, had made him fearful. He was fearful that everything he'd built for himself and his family could all be taken away (presumably by bad luck in business, strange quirks of fate, etc.) if he did not continue his relentless devotion to business. He rationalized that this hard work to provide for his wife, son, and daughter would replace what had been lacking from the deficient beginnings of his youth. Ironically, the focus it took to achieve this success came at a huge cost—dad time with his son and daughter—which left a void in Mr. Important's heart that he did not know how to remedy.

Not only was there simply no time for God in his life, but Mr. Important also could not see that his devotion to business equated to the very devotion to destruction of which God warns us. Of course, Mr. Important believed there was a God, albeit from his point of view, a fairly uninvolved one. He proudly proclaimed his membership and almost-every-Sunday (except during football season) attendance at one of the larger local churches. He did not, however, have any understanding of how intimately involved God is in our daily lives. To Mr. Important, the thought of the Son of God being intimately involved in our day-to-day lives—guiding our paths and shielding us from evil—was just plain ridiculous. Until now, Mr. Important had enjoyed relatively good health, was the CEO of a large international marketing firm, was in control of his company, and most importantly, was in control of his life. When I deal with patients in circumstances similar to Mr. Important's, God reveals to me that their anger and frustration are not really directed at me but rather at having to face the possibility of heart disease and losing control of their lives.

From his overall demeanor, it was clear to me that the door to Mr. Important's hardened heart was currently closed. Experience has taught me, however, that an opportunity to minister to his spiritual heart would open at some point in my care for him. The important thing was to diagnose and treat the problem that brought him into my office. The door to Mr. Important's spiritual heart might have been closed, but I was confident His guidance would provide the appropriate opportunity for further heart therapy.

Mr. Important had a frustrated look of "why me" on his face, and I began to explain to him in a straightforward but gentle manner that at five foot ten and 248 pounds, he desperately needed (a) a change of diet and (b) a regular exercise regimen. I told him he was experiencing classic symptoms of a heart problem, which was likely the reason behind the worsening of his pain or *discomfort*. Further, I went into detail about the arteriogram test that would give us needed insight into the underlying problems with his physical heart. He responded, however, not with questions about the test, but rather with an angry question about my suggestion for exercise.

"Why are we even talking about this exercise stuff when I've spent the past thirty minutes telling you about all this chest pressure?"

I took an encouraging tone and tried to explain that a steady diet of too many business lunches, dinners, drinks, desserts, and so on, had probably caught up with him like it can anyone. I suggested he approach these unhealthy habits and obstacles with the same resolve he had exhibited when he conquered his smoking habit years prior. Interestingly, however, I could tell the same resolve was suddenly nowhere to be found in him.

As I began to draw the office visit to a close with recommendations for further testing, much to my astonishment, Mr. Important abruptly answered his cell phone and began to explain to the caller that he was sorry for having canceled their very important meeting to have the nagging pressure in his chest checked out.

He nonchalantly ended the call and then returned his attention to me, as if it were a cue for me to continue. I was somewhat stunned at the rudeness of the interruption, but it almost made me laugh to keep from being angry at his attempt to control and minimize the seriousness of the moment.

I was doing my best to openly share with him that everyone encounters obstacles that are difficult to overcome alone—but fortunately, the Lord is always there for us to provide a pathway to success to overcome these obstacles. However, since I had already stirred his anger, I kept quiet and decided to let the Holy Spirit take charge of the message.

Mr. Important was struggling with not only serious physical heart problems, but also serious spiritual heart problems. His spiritual heart problems had likely been going on much longer than the physical ones—and were truly a more serious matter of life and death.

Further diagnostics and testing would soon define the physical heart problem responsible for interrupting Mr. Important's life, and hopefully, indicate an immediate fix to restore blood flow to his heart. *It will be much more difficult to repair his spiritual heart*, I thought to myself. Restoring his heart to its original position would be like putting a patch on the crack of a dam—sure to worsen at the first sign of pressure. Without also curing the spiritual heart, Mr. Important's physical heart would not stay repaired for long. The goal, then, would be to restore Mr. Important's heart to a new spiritual heart centered on a relationship with our Lord. Following His Word would help Mr. Important overcome the obstacles that prevented him from enjoying a heart-healthy lifestyle. Softening Mr. Important's spiritual heart to God's Word would be step number one, and it would open the only real gateway through which he could enjoy all the blessings that God has for his life.

We talked about the types of testing—in this case, coronary angiography—where we look at heart arteries by injecting dye to locate the likely blockage. We would then hopefully be able to utilize balloon and stent implantation technology to restore blood flow to his heart and repair his physical heart problem. By the nature of his progressively worsening symptoms, testing was needed very soon. I tried to convince Mr. Important that his schedule needed to be immediately changed to accommodate the tests. Remarkably, even in the face of potential death, Mr. Important chose to delay the arteriogram for eight full days in order to attend a shareholder meeting in California that he "simply could not miss." Even if he cared nothing for himself, I simply couldn't fathom his lack of consideration for his wife and family with his blatant defiance of the severity of his condition.

If there was any doubt prior to the procedure that God provides a shield of protection over our lives, it was visually evident with the results of Mr. Important's arteriogram. The blockage was so tight, blood was getting through, literally, only one drop at a time. How he kept from suffering a massive heart attack in the eight days prior to coming in on his own terms, truly only God knows. It reminded me that even when we make bad decisions that are potentially harmful to our lives, God still protects us. The culprit blockage was a complicated one for repair with a stent. However, the immediate fix of his physical heart blockage would be easier than the long-term prevention of worsening heart blockages. The continued hardening of his spiritual heart to God's Word would also be a difficult task to remedy.

In addition to the 99.9 percent blockage in the first portion of the front *important* artery to Mr. Important's heart, there was moderate diffuse buildup of cholesterol lining all three of his major arteries and branches. This would take significant effort at lifestyle changes, which he had objected to discussing at the first office visit, in order to minimize the chances of worsening heart blockages in the future. No change whatsoever would be possible, however, without first opening Mr. Important's eyes to the grace that God gives us when we open our hearts to His Word. The blockage was so tight we had to make room for a stent by opening the blockage first with a balloon. By opening the stent like scaffolding in the wall of Mr. Important's heart artery, he said it immediately made him feel better, even while he was lying on the cardiac catheterization table at the completion of the procedure.

As a business executive, Mr. Important was used to gathering the facts and acting upon them. So I decided that presenting him with the facts about heart disease would help him formulate a working plan to prevent the worsening of his heart disease. Before diving deeply into statistics, we discussed the most serious facts: heart disease is the number-one killer of men and women in this country (1 out of every 2.4 deaths), with nearly 12 million Americans suffering from cardiovascular disease. The leading causes of heart disease, I emphasized, are high blood pressure and other lifestyle-related issues—some of which he would be facing—like smoking, overeating, lack of exercise, elevated cholesterol, and diabetes. I also wanted to make sure that he understood that I was not the kind of doctor who would automatically put patients on medicine, as they would say, "to take care of the problem." A prescription is not necessarily the best shortcut to healing the heart, but he should be prepared to take some medicine, at least in the short term.

With the same unwavering commitment with which he scheduled lunches, dinners, meetings, and so on, Mr. Important would come to understand that everyone must schedule time for exercise. It does not matter what time of the day is chosen as long as the commitment to the chosen time is not compromised. Exercise has a way of relieving stress and rejuvenating our minds and bodies, making it well worth the effort. For me, the best time for exercise is at the end of the day, when I can consistently relieve stress and have time to fellowship with God as I run and work out. Simply stated, exercise must be a part of our everyday lives.

Mr. Important's diet would no doubt be a point of huge concern and ongoing struggle. The potentially life-threatening buildup of cholesterol in the major arteries of his heart—coupled with his perceived lack of time—meant he had to spend quality time with a nutritionist and religiously commit to strict adherence to the dietary recommendations. Before fixing the blockage in his heart, Mr. Important staunchly defended his thirty-year indulgence in the time-honored tradition of unhealthy business lunches and dinners. With a new lease on life and a genuine open-mindedness about God, Mr. Important had to blaze a mental trail to replace these traditions one by one with heart-healthy choices that would minimize calories and mitigate cholesterol.

There was also another change in store for Mr. Important—his relationships with his wife, children, friends, and business associates. The morning after his heart-cath procedure, Mr. Important confided in me that the natural stresses associated with his thirty-four-year marriage—as well as the relationship (or lack thereof) with his children—had weighed heavily on his chest. Relationships have to be nurtured, and by his own admission, he had always been driven to be superior at providing financially for the loved ones in his life, but rarely nurturing. Time spent at becoming, as he put it, "a self-made man" stole the time away from nurturing relationships with his wife and children.

The same control that Mr. Important exhibited at work was not at all evident in his life at home. Just like our relationships with our wives and children—as well as everyone else important in our lives— our relationships with God requires our best time, not time as an afterthought. As promised in Proverbs 8:17, "I love those who love me, and those who seek me find me." God wants us to seek Him daily and not just turn to him in times of desperation.

With a new, God-centered approach to life, work, and family, Mr. Important felt that he could handle—and ultimately conquer—the lifestyle changes. It had been only three short months since Mr. Important's stent procedure, when he came in for his first post-stent evaluation. In stark contrast to his attitude during our first office visit, his hardened heart had already begun softening to God's Word. In an unusual show of humility, he shared that he was fully aware that the success of lifestyle changes—and the long, healthy physical life that would result—could only be achieved with God being in his *new heart*. Mr. Important was finally beginning to understand that his relationship with God was far more important than the relationships he coveted with business colleagues and clients. In short, God was leading him to a point of understanding that a long-lasting change in his physical heart would first require a change in his spiritual heart. In addition to developing good habits to take the place of the bad ones that had plagued him most of his life, he knew he had to strive every day to follow the scriptural advice found in Colossians 3:17: "And whatever you do, whether in word or deed, do it all in the name of the Lord Jesus, giving thanks to God the Father through him." Mr. Important needed to triumph over his own self-important, self-indulgent, self-destructive heart by surrendering humbly to the God-honoring fact that any successes obtained in life come as a direct result of the talents and blessings bestowed upon our lives by our Creator.

I became a better cardiologist and hopefully a better man of God only after coming to the realization that I could not expertly fix any organ in the body—much less the most important organ in our bodies—without His blessings guiding my every effort.

Humbling our hearts and understanding that we are defined by who we are in Christ—not how successful we are in the world—is the key to all of us taking control of our lives.

The repair and initial progress made toward the healing of Mr. Important's physical heart was relatively routine and painless from a procedural standpoint. To stay physically healed, Mr. Important will have to stay committed to the lifestyle changes he has initiated and continue to stay committed to his spiritual heart changes by submitting daily to the truth of God's Word.

Chapter 2

A Joyful Heart

A cheerful heart is good medicine, but a crushed spirit dries up the bones.

—**Proverbs 17:22**

Almost everyone knows someone who has had a heart attack, stent, or coronary artery bypass operation. Many of those who stand out the most do not seem to deserve their fate. You almost never equate heart problems with a person who does not possess the traditional risk factors of age, hypertension, diabetes, elevated cholesterol, tobacco use, strong family history of coronary artery disease, sedentary lifestyle, or obesity. Logic dictates that the rule of life should be: if you should not have a heart problem, then you will not. However, experience dictates this is not always the case. The best we can ever do is put ourselves in a low-risk category and take care of ourselves physically to stay in that low-risk category. God never promised us a life free of health problems. Rather, He promised not to leave us, no matter what obstacle comes our way. In the face of His promise, it is nonetheless hard to live worry-free.

We need to understand that living in worry is the tool of the Devil—which leads me to the story of Mary Tallent's life. She initially saw me fifteen years ago for cardiac screening because of an abnormal ECG (electrocardiogram). I can remember almost everything about her initial evaluation in the office. At sixty-four years of age, the bright-eyed Mrs. Tallent was impeccably dressed and looked more like she was going to a luncheon with her friends at *The Club* instead of coming to a screening for heart problems. My first thought was, *this could be my mother.* Mrs. Tallent exercised religiously on a daily basis, enjoying every step of her three-mile brisk walk.

A retired beautician, Mrs. Tallent's smile, upright posture, dedication to exercise, and attention to her overall appearance made a heart attack seem almost foreign to her. Clearly, Mary's life was a picture-perfect example of the amazing parallel of spiritual and physical heart health.

People saw God's light through Mary's life and wanted what she had. But how do you tell if someone is as healthy on the inside as he or she appears on the outside? This is obviously a difficult question, as God is the only one who knows us so well that He knows every hair on our heads. Even when we are able to maintain a low-risk lifestyle, life is often full of uncertainties, where tomorrow is not guaranteed.

If we are—as the Scriptures encourage us—to live each day as if for the Lord, then Mrs. Tallent was a living testament to living as if for the Lord. She really did not feel that she should be in the doctor's office at all. Instead of being bound by worry about what could happen, she lived with the peace of God's grace, knowing that we are all sons and daughters of God and coheirs with Jesus. Mary stood firmly on Romans 8:17, which assures us that "Now if we are children, then we are heirs—heirs of God and co-heirs with Christ, if indeed we share in his sufferings in order that we may also share in his glory." God's love shone through her, and through these good times, Mrs. Tallent's faith made me certain she would maintain this attitude, even when difficult times came her way. She truly lived in the peace of knowing that God would never leave her. Mary also lived with the knowledge that everything she was doing from a diet and exercise standpoint would serve her well throughout her life.

No matter how busy one's day, thirty minutes of exercise to unwind and fellowship with God is a stress relief, clearing both the mind and body of the day's toxins and mental clutter. There is an enormous sense of pride and accomplishment—even when we are physically and mentally tired and emotionally pushed—that we still discipline ourselves to maintain the body God gave us. You cannot wait to exercise when you "feel like" exercising, because it's not necessarily an activity you ever "feel like" doing. How many days do you feel like getting out of bed and going to work but go anyway? The aches and pains of life are enough to discourage us from getting out and working at a healthy life. Knowing God commands us to be good stewards of the body He gave us, we follow His command, which in turn makes it easier to overcome the obstacles to a healthy lifestyle. Moreover, as Christians—knowing that it pleases God's heart—we should seek to honor Him by following His command to improve our physical health, especially during times of difficulty that we will assuredly face.

Mrs. Tallent's testing confirmed her low risk. Her blood pressure remained well-controlled with very little medication combined with her daily exercise regimen. Each spring for fifteen years she came into the office for her yearly follow-up with the fresh outlook of a new year. It is no wonder that on a beautiful Saturday morning in early May when Mary awoke with significant chest discomfort, she immediately dismissed it as muscle soreness from pruning some tree branches in her garden the day before. Gardening brought Mrs. Tallent immense joy, as it was the one lifelong activity she and Mr. Tallent had shared together until his death from a stroke five years earlier. Mary clearly worked for her good health, even on days when she did not feel like exercising. However, on this particular Saturday, Mary's daughter Elaine knew instinctively that her mom truly was not feeling well when Mary skipped her routine three-mile walk. Elaine could not remember the last time her mother had missed her walk.

Could it have been that Mary's body was trying to interrupt the occurrence of a heart attack? Later that day, the discomfort seemed to improve, and Mrs. Tallent went about her business—even baking numerous batches of goodies for the church picnic the next day. Later that evening while showering, the discomfort recurred and gripped her in a far more serious way, including a sudden wave of nausea and lightheadedness. Realizing the severity of the symptoms, Mrs. Tallent had the presence of mind to slowly lower herself to the floor of the bathroom and crawl to the telephone to call her daughter, who summoned the paramedics to Mrs. Tallent's home. On the paramedics' arrival, Mrs. Tallent was pale and short of breath, and she had broken into a cold sweat. She was still having chest discomfort, and it was becoming harder to breathe. The nausea didn't subside even when lying down, causing her to feel as though she were going to pass out at any moment. On arrival at her local small-town emergency room, she was taken to the chest pain center, and her clinical situation was quickly assessed. Following blood tests and an electrocardiogram, treatment was initiated to relieve Mary's symptoms.

Hearing the emergency-room physician declare, "Mrs. Tallent, you are having a heart attack," felt like a dream—albeit a dream made less real from the stupor of the morphine she was given for the pain.

"That can't be true," she mumbled. "I take excellent care of my heart."

Even though the physician assured her it was true, Mrs. Tallent did not become discouraged. The surreal nature of the helicopter ride to the cardiac cath lab served to heighten her feeling that this wasn't really happening. With heart attacks, time equals muscle damage. The longer the time taken to open up the artery, the more damage will likely occur—which could result in a worse outcome, or even death. The helicopter arrived at our hospital, and the staff's sole purpose focused upon interrupting this heart attack in order to save Mary's life.

Angiography confirmed that which shouldn't have been happening—a completely closed heart artery was causing a life-threatening heart attack in the front wall of her heart. Was it something that Mary did to deserve this? Did God stop loving her? At no time did Mrs. Tallent allow this thought to enter her mind. Even though there was confusion in her eyes, there was absolutely no fear whatsoever. Mrs. Tallent exhibited the same radiant, unshakable confidence that she was in God's loving hands as she had been for the previous fifteen years of excellent health. Looking back on that evening, I'm not sure I'll ever witness a moment that would better illustrate the confidence and comfort alluded to by David in Psalm 23:4: "Even though I walk through the valley of the shadow of death, I will fear no evil, for you are with me; your rod and your staff, they comfort me."

As she was lying on the cath table, she looked up at me and quietly asked, "Dr. Constantine, how could it be my heart?" Then, before I could respond, she answered her own question by paraphrasing my signature answer to all patients ... "I forgot," she whispered. "It's always the heart, isn't it?"

There was a sense of urgency, as always when someone comes to the cath lab having a heart attack. Everyone carried out their duties swiftly as we worked to open the blocked artery with a balloon and subsequently repair the artery with a stent. It was amazing to see the relief in Mrs. Tallent's face when the balloon restored the pathway of blood to her heart and immediately, her chest discomfort went away. Her face went from grim to peaceful in a matter of only a moment or two.

God warns us the Devil works at times through our physical illnesses to introduce doubt and fear, which was precisely how Mrs. Tallent would be attacked now that she had faced death from interruption of blood flow to her most vital organ. There were no other blockages, but _the damage_ remained in Mary's mind.

After building a strong patient relationship with Mrs. Tallent through the years, I was confident that she would not lose heart through the Devil's relentless assault and would work hard to recover and be a testament to God's healing powers in her life. No other organ in our bodies is given the importance of the heart in keeping us physically and spiritually healthy. I was confident that God would use Mrs. Tallent's near-death experience as a beautiful example of how someone can heal physically and spiritually from an attack on his or her most important organ. God gives hearts the same importance in spiritual health as well as physical health. Experience had taught me that despite her standing on a solid foundation, it would take a _healing_ of Mrs. Tallent's spiritual heart as she battled the lies of the Devil that she would always have a heart problem.

Physically, her continued hard work of a nutritious diet and daily exercise discipline would also be necessary to help her recover and return to the same levels of activity as she adhered to before the heart attack.

God talks of health and healing, and also faith and believing, which are the actions on our parts necessary to receive this healing. God wants us to receive this healing, but it will take faith and action on our parts for this to occur. The Devil's attack tried to steal the joy Mrs. Tallent had in her heart. Yet knowing the all-sufficient comfort of God's Word, she was able to drown out his lies and continue to strive for the promise of a long, healthy life. Amazingly, in spite of having endured a serious heart attack, the area of muscle damage was minimal. Testing confirmed this divine healing of the area, and any heart-muscle damage from the heart attack was no longer present. This healing—coupled with the fact that there was also no other blockage in the remaining coronary arteries—made it nearly certain that Mrs. Tallent's physical healing would be lasting.

Since the heart attack did not result in physical death, she refused to die spiritually. Her constant nurturing of her spiritual heart health enabled her to persevere through the difficult times. Despite her firm footing on God's Word, Mary felt the battle to successfully restore a healthy spiritual heart was much more difficult than her battle to restore a healthy physical heart.

Sure, there were moments of discouragement, especially within the first few weeks of her return home. As expected, at times self-pity crept into her thoughts. There were good days and bad days when alone at home. Occasionally, she even found herself preoccupied with anxiety when every pain brought to mind that it might be another heart attack. But overall, Mrs. Tallent overcame the down times by reminding herself that a spiritually healthy heart not only leads to everlasting life in heaven, but allows us to experience His love and healing hand here in our earthly lives.

It was now a new season in Mary's life. Six months after the heart attack, to stay encouraged on her continuing road to recovery, Mrs. Tallent would find uplifting Bible passages that reminded her of what God wants for her life. It was a constant battle, but Mary knew that she had to maintain a relentless focus on the things she knew God wanted in her life. "Look to the LORD and his strength; seek his face always" (1 Chronicles 16:11) became one of her daily guideposts to understanding the true source of her strength. She knew that her heart was healed, and that to stay healthy, God would do what she could not. Her strong faith allowed her to experience divine healing. The day of her heart attack seemed so long ago in Mary's mind, and now looked like it never even happened.

Today, she works in her garden with even more enthusiasm than before. The warmth of her smile is just as radiant as ever. And most importantly, her faith in God is undoubtedly stronger than the first time I saw her shining face in my office. God never promised that we would not encounter spiritual and physical troubles in our lives, but He reassured us that *He would never leave us* and would always be there to help us through our difficult times. Although Mrs. Tallent's heart-health problems were not deserved by worldly standards, she emerged a more beautiful and confident follower of Christ, who would now be able to witness firsthand to Christ's healing powers in her life and point to the Savior of all mankind as the eternal keeper of her heart. "Be joyful always; pray continually; give thanks in all circumstances, for this is God's will for you in Christ Jesus." (1 Thessalonians 5:16–18).

Chapter 3

Addiction

For the grace of God that brings salvation has appeared
to all men. It teaches us to say "No" to ungodliness and
worldly passions, and to live self-controlled, upright and
godly lives in this present age, while we wait for the blessed
hope—the glorious appearing of our great God and Savior,
Jesus Christ, who gave himself for us to redeem us from
all wickedness and to purify for himself a people that are
his very own, eager to do what is good.

—Titus 2:11–14

Everyone in life battles addictions—some worse than others—and no one
traverses this minefield unaffected. Most people who are not troubled
with drugs and/or alcohol would say they have no addictions, but if we
truly examine our hearts, there is always something that has our focus.
Addictions take many forms, and just because one may be mind-altering
while another may not, they both can be harmful to our health. The Devil
knows this and uses these addictions to distract us and keep us down, to
keep us from the truth of how God sees us and what He wants for our lives.

My cardiology practice reflects life—most people seeing a heart
doctor struggle with the most common obstacles to a long, healthy life.
The struggles with tobacco/nicotine, sugar/desserts, cholesterol, fried
foods, boxed/bagged/processed foods, lack of exercise, or stress and
anger are seemingly—either individually or collectively—a part of the

everyday lives of nearly every patient who walks into my office. Just like a cross section of society, there are those I see in the office who have the added burden of addictions to drugs and/or alcohol to turn their focus away from God's plan for their lives.

On my first encounter with Jacob (as in Jacob the deceiver in the Old Testament), it was easy to see that many things had a hold on his life. Amazingly, at only forty-one years old, he looked dreadfully older. He was average in height at five feet eleven inches, but extremely thin. With sunken cheeks, hollow eyes, and twiglike arms and legs, he tipped the scales at just under 136 pounds. Obviously, when it came to feeding his body the proper fuel required to stay healthy, Jacob placed it at the very lowest level on his list of life's priorities.

Upon entering the exam room, I found it, literally, nearly impossible to breathe from the stench of the stale cigarette smoke emanating from his clothes. In fact, I was concerned about how long it would take for the stale odor from his cigarettes to dissipate, so that the next patient entering the exam room didn't find himself or herself gasping for breath. On the subject of his smoking, Jacob spoke deliberately but was selectively truthful in his admission to smoking a mixture of two to three packs of cigarettes per day and marijuana—both of which he claimed calmed his nerves.

His admission to "a couple of beers a day," however, fell a bit shy on the truth meter. The extreme levels of consumption of all of the other bad stuff in his life led me to believe that he was likely consuming far more than a couple of beers each day. He pronounced that he was "done with cocaine," claiming to have used that drug for the very last time a couple of weeks earlier. Yet I could tell in his heart, there was little if any commitment behind his claim.

His five-day-old beard was scraggly and scruffy and so was his hair. A mouthful of decay in the teeth he wanted to keep—along with his eyes that were sunken into bony sockets, as if protruding into his head—spoke of a man who paid little attention to the needs of his body. It would be hard to guess the last time the dirty, tattered, worn clothes had been washed. Tattoos covered nearly every exposed inch of skin on Jacob's chest, back, and arms, truly making him look as though he were of a different, multicolor race.

The tattoo symbolism spoke of death and destruction, fire and hell, as if there were a need to remind anyone how far away from God he was. These observations told more about Jacob than anything he could have said about the *state of his heart*.

Jacob was on "disability," apparently due to his "bad back," which seemingly did not prevent him from making a little extra money doing odd jobs like painting and light yard work around town. When he told me one of his regular odd jobs was cleaning a man's hogpen for cash, it further revealed the grip addiction had on his life. *Here's a man*, I thought, *who has resorted to cleaning up after the lowest-of-the-lowest bottom feeders on the earth in order to feed his dependency on drugs.* His rough, dirty hands looked as if this *disabled* man was *able* when it came to things important to his destruction. Jacob told me his first wife had left him and he had not seen his two children—now teenagers—in over ten years. Of course, he reasoned that he had made occasional attempts to see them over the years, but as they got older (and wiser), he just quit trying because, as he said, "they made me feel like a stranger whenever I was with them." In his mind, it was clear he was not at all at fault for the strained relationship with his ex-wife and children. Jacob was in the office alone but had a fiancée who worked at the local factory in his small town.

I am not sure why Jacob finally came in to see me—he didn't really know himself; he just thought he was "dying." His history was difficult to sort out. Everything I asked, he had experienced: chest pain, chest pressure—sharp and dull, at rest or with exertion. He said, "It doesn't matter what I'm doing. It even wakes me up from a dead sleep, and can last a few minutes or all day—and it seems to be getting worser all the time." Remarkably, he claimed to be short of breath all the time but doubted the cigarettes had anything to do with that. He complained of "butterflies" in his chest and said that at times, he felt like his heart was "running away and flip-flopping." He was always dizzy and frequently felt like he was going to pass out for no apparent reason—completely discounting the possibility that the combination of cocktails and cocaine would knock over even the strongest of men.

To hear him recount the severity of his symptoms, it was surprising we did not have to rush him to the hospital to save his life at that moment. Jacob characterized these symptoms as going on for years, mistakenly thinking the extraordinary length of time made it more likely to be coming from his physical heart. In reality, the length of time told a story more consistent with his spiritual heart problem. The true problem was not stemming from Jacob's physical heart but the current state of his spiritual heart. To ascertain the condition of Jacob's heart after years of self-abuse and neglect, it was clear we would need to proceed with testing to check for evidence of premature heart disease and any possible heart damage.

It is well known how tobacco use, sedentary lifestyle, and improper diet negatively impact our hearts and bodies—but cocaine and alcohol abuse can also have disastrous consequences to physical heart health. Cocaine has been known to cause and accelerate premature atherosclerosis, spasms of heart arteries, life-threatening arrhythmias (abnormal heart rhythms), and elevated blood pressure. Alcohol, predominantly in excess, can cause weakening of the heart muscle and decrease in heart function, which can lead to life-threatening arrhythmias.

Because of Jacob's risky lifestyle, abnormal ECG, and multiple symptoms, I felt proceeding directly to angiography/cardiac catheterization to actually visualize the heart arteries and the heart size and function was the necessary next step to accurately determine the current state of his physical heart.

Despite countless reasons for Jacob to have a severely diseased heart, amazingly, the arteriogram/cardiac catheterization revealed only moderate diffuse atherosclerosis lining his heart arteries, with normal heart size and function.

There was certainly evidence of premature atherosclerosis of his heart arteries, but not bad enough to decrease blood flow to the heart muscle and cause the symptoms Jacob was experiencing. Once again, God's grace and love were revealed by this finding. In a situation where Jacob could not do any more to cause harm, Jacob's heart was relatively healthy, with no damage from the years of abusive lifestyle. To change his life and *change his heart*, Jacob would have to change his spiritual heart. To retard progression of this premature coronary artery disease and live a long, healthy life, Jacob would have to *change his life*.

It did not take long to see how he was not ready to accept responsibility to change. He was an easy target for Satan—and his battles with drugs and alcohol served as a huge bull's-eye on his back by clouding his mind from the truth as described in 1 Peter 5:8: "Be self-controlled and alert. Your enemy the devil prowls around like a roaring lion looking for someone to devour." There was very little the Devil needed to do to distract him; Jacob was doing enough all by himself.

In order to start the process of change, Jacob would first need to know that God sees us differently than we see ourselves. As God told Samuel, "...The LORD does not look at the things man looks at. Man looks at the outward appearance, but the LORD looks at the heart" (1 Sam. 16:7). We confuse our defects with our identities, making it hard to see what God sees. It would take Jacob knowing His Word to find out the truth of what God says to battle those lies. It is hard to battle the lies of the Devil—the father of lies—without knowing the truth of what God says about us. It would take a relationship with our Lord to know what He says and to change Jacob's heart to see what He sees. Moreover, it would take surrendering his life to Christ in order for Jacob to develop the strength to overcome his addictions.

Admittedly, this person, Jacob, sounds extreme, and although he is real, I can almost hear many readers saying, "This is not me; this message doesn't apply to me." But in reality, there are many Jacobs out there with drug and/or alcohol addictions who hide things better but are truly burdened with the same struggles. There are still others who may not only face the burden of alcohol or drug abuse but also such seemingly *innocent* addictions as gluttony, pornography, techno-addictions, and so on, all of which interfere with their walk with God. These addictions, while not necessarily against man's law, can prevent us from enjoying a long, healthy life and heart by being against God's law.

Fast-forward thirty days ... and here sat another Jacob—Jacob the electrician. Ironically, this Jacob sat in the same office, the same exam room, in the same small town, for evaluation of chest pain. To look at him, he was no different than any of us—though certainly by outward appearances much different than the previous Jacob. As a testament to all needing God's grace, he too battled drugs and alcohol in his life. Jacob had a lucrative electrical contracting business until cocaine abuse caused his life to spiral out of control. Cocaine was his god, and he worshipped it fervently. Use of the destructive drug consumed every waking moment of his life. He lost nearly everything of monetary value that he had worked so hard for and had come to the point of losing his business and home. His family, frustrated with his unwillingness to put them ahead of his cocaine, had nearly left him. Everything important to him was slipping through his fingers. Outwardly, Jacob hid his demon from everyone, with no one ever suspecting he was a slave to the corrosive chemical that had contributed significantly to eroding his business to the brink of bankruptcy.

He was about to be exposed, as it is referenced in John 3:20: "Everyone who does evil hates the light, and will not come into the light for fear that his deeds will be exposed." Even though Jacob knew about God, he did not really *know* Him, and certainly did not know the healing power of Jesus. Thankfully, Jacob's wife had faith in Jesus, stuck with Jacob during his struggles, and at his lowest point brought him to a Wednesday night church service focused on recovery. A preacher spoke of God's perfect love and grace, and Jacob felt the power of the Holy Spirit and that night was a changed man. By the passion of his witness, I knew that healing had begun that life-changing night in Jacob's heart. This amazing transformation led Jacob to freedom from the stronghold of cocaine addiction, yet he could not stop smoking—a seemingly weaker demon.

Now, sitting in the same exam room, for virtually the same reasons and some of the same symptoms, I found myself treating a different Jacob ... Jacob the electrician. Like Jacob the deceiver, Jacob the electrician was also noticing symptoms that became concerning to him. He was experiencing chest pressure and shortness of breath carrying equipment at work and feared it was his heart. Truth is, these symptoms that make us wonder if it is our hearts are not unique to these two Jacobs; they could have been experienced by any of us at any time.

Although the issues were the same, there was a sharp contrast in almost everything else about the two Jacobs. The latter Jacob's heart for Jesus was clear, and his desire for recovery was evident—much different from the first Jacob, who was still a target for Satan's deception. The story of how Jacob the electrician quit using cocaine was vastly different than the previous Jacob's story. No one can change on his or her own without the transforming power of Jesus.

Jacob the electrician overcame his addictions because Jesus *changed his heart*—unlike Jacob the deceiver, who quit because he *ran out of money*.

As hard as it is to believe, the power that nicotine addiction had on Jacob the electrician was harder for him to overcome than that of cocaine. From society's point of view, it is strange how we are more accepting of someone like Jacob the electrician's struggles with cigarettes than with his cocaine use. Utilizing classic guilt rationalization to quiet the voice in our consciences, we tell ourselves, "He is really just a person like me, facing the same things I am facing." Even though God had clearly lit the path to freedom from the electrician's cocaine addiction, the persistence of the deceiver to lie to him clouded Jacob's mind, making it impossible to find the same pathway to freedom from his nicotine addiction.

The Devil speaks lies to your mind in hopes of gaining permanent ownership of your heart. Guarding your heart is one of the most important points of vigilance any Christian can maintain. It can only be done by knowing what God says about you. The Devil is the father of lies and wants us to dwell on and live in the negative. There is no truth in Satan—when he lies, he speaks his native language. He likes to keep us down, lying that you will never change. His lies are so convincing, we confuse our defects with our identities, making it hard to see what God sees in us. God sees us differently than we see ourselves, and it takes knowing His Word to find out the truth of our true identities. We have to fellowship with God daily, constantly renewing our minds to battle the lies of Satan.

Society's utter disregard for the first Jacob's lifestyle and hardened heart makes it difficult to sympathize with him and his struggles with addiction. Yet the same forgiving grace is needed by all, making these Jacobs like all of us in more ways than we would all care to admit.

Just as sin in God's eye is all the same, we all have addictions that can distract us from His chosen path for our lives. As a cardiologist, I have been blessed with an amazing platform to reveal the truth about God's healing powers no matter the addiction, issue, problem, or lifestyle. There is no problem too great, no lifestyle too bad, nothing we have done too much for our Lord to overcome. Similarly, there is no addiction too small if it is blocking our fellowship with God, that we do not need His help to overcome. Our first step in overcoming these addictions—large or small—is surrendering them to God. I often hear people fall back on the "My addiction is not as bad as his or hers" excuse, or "There's no way I can exercise; I have a bad back" excuse … or my all-time favorite: "I'm never going to be thin … I'm fat and that's just the way I am." All of these are excuses, and all of them require taking the all-important first step to surrender.

The difficulty in *curing* Jacob the deceiver was his hardened heart, which prevented the seed of change from taking root in his life to free him from his addictions. It became difficult to sift through the lies of his lifestyle while battling both his symptoms and his *victim mentality*. While soaking himself in self-pity, he chalked up his current situation to everything except his free will and poor choices. We fuel Satan's power when we allow his lies to resonate in our hearts as truth.

By contrast, I immediately knew by the testimony in his heart that Jacob the electrician was committed to overcoming drug addiction. The door to his softened heart was opened, and he had already started the process of healing. His heart was not hardened—which is always the hardest obstacle to recovery—and he was receptive to God's Word. Jacob found himself in agreement with God's truth, which would hopefully open the door to his fully submitting to following God's plan to help him overcome the obstacles that stood in the way of his healthy heart.

Even having overcome a cocaine addiction, it was now strangely more difficult for Jacob to overcome a habit most of us might consider easier to kick. In the process of recovery, we try to negotiate with God, trying to selectively apply His Word to our lives. It is human nature to want to control our lives and hold on to something, refusing to fully surrender to God.

"I stopped using cocaine, but I can't stop smoking," Jacob stated in a half matter-of-fact, half dejected manner. Other patients who smoke commonly say, "I used to smoke two packs per day, but I've cut back a whole lot, Doc," hoping to get a complimentary response on their cutback. "I don't even smoke a pack a day," they proudly proclaim. Others typically say, "Ever since I slowed down on my smoking, I have gained so much weight"—as if weight gain were out of their control. Still others rationalize, "I can't exercise because of arthritis in my knees, hips, feet, ankles, and back," as excuses for being overweight. With a giant measure of self-pity, they also say, "Furthermore, exercise can be darn near impossible when you have fibromyalga as badly as I do."

We, as Jacobs, are really asking for a compromise—which is how all of us try to bargain with God in hopes that He will compromise His uncompromising Word. Following God's instruction is not easy, but when we open our hearts—and stop trying to care for our temples in a manner that best suits our selfish motives—He gives us the strength to do the things we find difficult to do on our own.

Change is a process, and not usually immediate. It is necessary to live our lives in accordance with God, and eventually we will get to the place He wants us to go. Our heads need to come into agreement with our hearts. Ask God to let that which is in our hearts come out of our mouths and follow His Word in our lives.

Proverbs 17:24 is an appropriate reminder that "A discerning man keeps wisdom in view, but a fool's eyes wander to the ends of the earth."

Change is a process but starts out with one step. Recovery starts with the first step of surrender—focusing on God's power, not your own. And finally, change always requires God's power and strength. Philippians 4:13 reminds us, "I can do everything through him who gives me strength."

People come to me wanting and expecting me to *fix their hearts*, but I cannot. Most times I can only heal the physical problem at hand; for complete healing, God says we have to be transformed. I cannot even fix me, much less someone else. Like all of God's children, I need the same transforming power of Jesus in my life in order to make a lasting change. Like Nicodemus in the New Testament, we need a new birth, *a new heart*.

The first Jacob in this chapter continued to follow a recipe of cocaine, cigarettes, alcohol, poor nutritional choices, and sedentary lifestyle of "sitting around piddling"—which resulted in a severe heart attack six months later that left him with considerable heart-muscle damage.

In this very short period of time, his coronary artery disease had progressed from moderate diffuse to severe diffuse, and was particularly bad in two separate arteries, which required stents to interrupt the heart attack and save his physical life. The severe damage ultimately required a defibrillator—a device implanted like a pacemaker designed to shock his heart out of life-threatening arrhythmia (an electrical problem that is common to severely damaged and scarred heart muscle). Jacob's physical heart damage now matched his spiritually damaged heart. By the amazing grace of God, Jacob is still alive physically and has time to come alive spiritually to experience God's grace both here on earth and in heaven.

Amazingly, even after all of his physical and mental pain and suffering, he continued to use and abuse God's gift of life, refusing to soften his hardened heart.

Jacob the electrician struggled with total surrender, bargaining with God that at least he stopped the illegal drug use while continuing to smoke. Even with firsthand knowledge of Jesus' power in helping to overcome his drug addiction, he found it hard to draw upon the same transforming power to break his reliance on the socially accepted addiction of smoking. The difference was that he knew the truth of God's power in his life, but just needed to focus on His guidance to fully develop and renew his spiritual heart. Jacob the electrician, too, developed severe substernal chest discomfort that made him feel certain that he was, as he proclaimed, "havin' a big heart attack."

Flown by helicopter out of the small-town emergency room, Jacob #2 was rushed to the chest pain center. He underwent emergency angiography, which revealed minor blockages and no heart attack. This life-threatening scare was all Jacob needed in order to change his life and give up cigarettes the same way he gave up cocaine. The same Lord who had saved him once would save him again. The work of restoring his business had led Jacob away from his daily fellowship with God. The pride he felt in overcoming his cocaine addiction—coupled with the twelve-hour days of resurrecting his business—distracted him from his walk with God. *After all*, he thought, *why after reading the Bible several times over, do I need to read it again?* We need constant reminders of what God says about us. He reveals something different to us on each encounter with His Word. The more we see and hear God's grace and love, the more we know of God's plan for us. Jeremiah 29:11 reassures us, "'For I know the plans I have for you,' declares the LORD, 'plans to prosper you and not to harm you, plans to give you hope and a future.'"

With careful and constant pruning and molding, Jacob—and all of us—will change and become the ones God intends us to be.

We are to focus on the process, not perfection. We are never going to become perfect, and yet, if the process becomes our way of life, we get as close to perfection as possible.

Chapter 4

Searching

But seek his kingdom, and these things will be given to you as well.

—**Luke 12:31**

As we go through life, we search—for the right school, the right career, the right mate ... but are we ever really content? Will we be content when we earn enough money, or perhaps attain a high or lofty-enough position at work? Or could it be when we have been married twenty-five years, with the children grown and out of the house? We have all been through the "when I get through this phase, then I will be happy" times in our lives, rather than enjoying the moment for what it is.

As long as we are searching *for things*, there is a high likelihood we will never find true contentment. We are all searching for our purposes in life, but many times try searching so hard using our own strengths that we miss the true path God desires for us to follow. God reminds us in Proverbs 3:6 that we cannot do the work of God apart from Him: "in all your ways acknowledge him, and he will make your paths straight." He also promises in Psalm 23:3 to guide us and bring us to our appointed goals: "he restores my soul. He guides me in the paths of righteousness for his name's sake." The wind in our hearts is His spirit, which allows us to push forward and carry out the desires of our lives.

God addresses contentment with us in Philippians 4:11: "I am not saying this because I am in need, for I have learned to be content whatever the circumstances." Many of the patients I see are not content; they are caught up in the world's race to keep up, searching for the wrong things to give them peace. This definitely has an effect on our physical bodies and affects how we feel.

For the most part, the enormous stress we internalize when trying to do things on our own has to come out, and usually does with a conglomeration of symptoms that can understandably lead one to think it is his or her heart. Assuredly the heart is the center of our physical and emotional existences and reacts to the physical and emotional stresses in our lives, which can truly make us feel sick—and in some cases, actually make us sick.

This feeling and being sick are what Joanne began to worry about after experiencing chest pain for several hours. It seemed to worsen as the afternoon went on. My first encounter with Joanne—a reasonably healthy forty-eight-year-old female—was in the ER at 5:07 p.m. Her husband, John, was understandably concerned and never left her side. Joanne knew she needed medical attention after several hours of indigestion-type chest discomfort, which began gradually some time after lunch with clients, worsening until, as she put it, it was "like something was squeezing the life out of my chest."

Many possible causes for the discomfort fluttered around in Joanne's mind as she tried to figure out what was going on. Surely *it couldn't be her heart*, she wondered, yet she thought of her friend Abigail, who had a heart attack a couple of months earlier. "No way," she said to herself. "Abigail was a two-pack-a-day smoker." As quickly as it came to her, Joanne shook the thought out of her head. Could it have been the Mediterranean chicken breast she had for lunch—sautéed with garlic, oregano, and pepper spices—or could it be the stress and pressure of her job? She loved the fact that she was finally *free to find her purpose in life* in corporate America—a paying career that had been put on hold for years as she birthed and raised children. Joanne did not realize that pursuing what she thought she wanted would create so much stress. Could it be muscular from the weekend spent sprucing up the yard from winter's destruction and spring's new growth?

Despite the many possibilities that raced through Joanne's mind, she was certain it couldn't have been her heart. Joanne waited at home, took two aspirins and something over the counter for indigestion, and went to rest on the couch. As the discomfort did not let up and Joanne became short of breath and broke out in a cold sweat, she "knew something wasn't right." Panic set in, and Joanne began to feel as if she were going to pass out. The graying of her vision forced Joanne to lie down on the bedroom hardwood floor. Trying to sit up brought on what she described as "a feeling of doom," so Joanne lay there terrified, not knowing what to do next. She finally crawled, head down, to the phone and frantically called John, who rushed home from work and insisted they hurry to the ER to, as he said, "make sure it wasn't her heart."

Joanne's appearance clearly was not typical for most people having a heart attack; she looked out of place to be seeing a cardiologist in the ER. She really did not appear as sick as the life-threatening situation she potentially faced. But the ER physicians had begun treatment, starting the process of making her better. There was no gray in her blonde hair, professionally coifed by Spiridon, a well-known makeup artist, proudly from Corfu, Greece, who attended to the country music stars of Nashville. It was evident that Joanne pampered herself with manicures, makeup accents, and massage services, which her membership in the day spa afforded. From a cardiologist's assessment, many things made it unlikely that the problem was Joanne's heart. She had no reason to have heart disease. Her age made it unlikely to be her heart, and Joanne had none of the traditional risk factors of heart disease—no hypertension, no diabetes, no hyperlipidemia. Joanne's family history was significant for cancer but not heart disease. Furthermore, Joanne boasted "I never tried cigarettes in my life." Other than an appendectomy twenty years earlier, there were no hospitalizations or medical procedures unless you count procedures done to preserve her youth—the Botox injections, lip augmentations, and even breast augmentations.

She tried to eat right, concerned inwardly for keeping her body in shape, without really professing she did so to try to stay healthy. Joanne was far from sedentary as she was always on the go. However, her usual routine was not committed to forty-five minutes of daily exercise. She did enjoy exercising when she had—or actually made—time, going to classes, yoga, and Pilates. Joanne sometimes power walked, yet always with her friends—primarily as a social outing in order to multitask and catch up with her "girlfriends." It appeared she was more concerned about her appearance than her health. Like many of us, the aches, pains, and fatigue of middle-aged life were creeping in; however, Joanne was considered very healthy. From a cardiologist's perspective, if she were not wearing the hospital gown, it would have been very difficult to tell that Joanne was indeed the patient.

However, in the ER, the ECG confirmed what should not be happening; for *no reason, Joanne was the patient*. She was having a heart attack.

Contentment was always elusive for Joanne, and her life had been a pattern of searching for her purpose in life. She was always busy, and she admitted that staying busy seemed to help her fill a void in her life. Joanne came to thrive on this full schedule. Ironically, not only did this staying busy try to cover up the emptiness in her life, but it inadvertently served as a distraction to the true path God wanted her to follow. Joanne needed to fill up every minute of her day with friends and activities, which made it impossible to spend time alone with God. There was no true contentment where she was. Rather than living with continuous joy during each stage of her life, Joanne's vision was clouded by her exhaustive efforts to find her purpose.

After college and before having children, she held several jobs, but none gave her a sense of fulfillment. Soon she and John began their family, and all her attempts at developing a career had to be put on hold to raise their four wonderful children. Instead of trusting God for guidance and peace during this part of her life, Joanne just went through the motions, "holding on," as she describes it, subconsciously putting contentment on hold until the kids were gone to college and this part of her life was complete. She did not want time to pass, but down deep, she would envision how her "life would take off" when this chapter was complete. When the kids were older, in high school and college, it was time for Joanne to find what was missing all these years. In 1 Peter 3:11, God instructs us to seek peace, "…he must seek peace and pursue it"… but she was going to pursue things missing in her life to find peace. John's success had them financially settled. Joanne wanted a career to fill a void, not for the money, but because *something was missing*.

Especially since Joanne did not really need the money, she soon found the success of her job to be okay, but it still did not fill the void in her heart. She still felt empty as she tried to fulfill her life with her power, not God's.

There was a time in Joanne's life at age forty when she felt unfulfilled with her job as a stay-at- home mom and battled feelings of depression, anxiety, and fear that she would become her mother and miss out on her career. She always felt sorry for her mother, who as she lamented, "never did anything with her life" as a stay-at-home mom who lovingly raised Joanne, her brother, and her sisters. She vowed that this was not going to happen to her.

Making matters worse, John, a kind and loving father, was always traveling because of his job as a national sales account manager, which added to the stress and drudgery of Joanne feeling as though it just was not fair that she was assuming the duties of a single parent much of the time.

It was at that time in her life that Joanne saw a cardiologist in the office because she *knew something was wrong with her heart* when she began to develop palpitations, rapid heartbeat, chest pain, fatigue, and shortness of breath. True to His Word, God instructs us that we are not alone. "The LORD is close to the brokenhearted and saves those who are crushed in spirit" (Psalms 34:18). Joanne was not then, and would not be now, alone in her situation.

In the same manner as Joanne had done eight years prior, many women see me in the office with similar complaints, certain that they have a heart problem. Females, from young to middle-aged, bear heavy burdens of the world's stresses with their jobs, families, and financial pressures. While the specifics may vary, the underlying issues of distraction, searching, and lack of contentment are always the same. These women come in with a wide array of symptoms that mimic heart problems resulting from something missing in their personal life— whether at home, work, school, or play. Like Joanne, their chest pain and shortness of breath are difficult for them to describe and are very unpredictable.

Their chest pain has multiple qualities—both sharp and dull—in several locations of the chest, back, shoulders, and neck; it has no relation to activity and often seems more pronounced at the end of the day. The duration of the pain is always variable and sometimes, as they emphatically proclaim, it "won't go away for days," which erroneously makes them think it is most likely coming from the heart. Similarly, the shortness of breath is with and without activity. It usually sounds more like tiredness and fatigue; they describe it as if they "can't get a deep breath." Despite feeling short of breath, this does not seem to interrupt their ability to carry on their activities without interruption. They commonly describe a "flutter like butterflies" in their chests and frequent skips in their heartbeat that "drive them crazy." This fluttering at times leads to dizziness and a feeling as if they might pass out.

The only pattern to these symptoms is that stress and worry seem to bring them on and they intensify with increasing emotional stresses. These patients, like Joanne, see a cardiologist in the office and are living on their emotions, which can lie and deceive, rather than on God's Word. They come in *knowing it must be their hearts*, and in many ways it is. Truthfully, almost all of the women I see in this situation do not have a physical heart problem and will never have a heart attack. Their hearts are only reacting to the external and internal stresses of life. Unknown to them, these stresses are draining away their strength and joy and affecting every cell in their bodies.

Contentment is lacking. True contentment is something learned, not acquired. It is independent of our circumstances and is all tied to Christ. When we do not have our priorities in order and *chase after things* to make us happy, there is unrest in our souls, which leads us to believe that we are sick. Despite a low risk of heart disease in these patients, testing is necessary, if for nothing else than for the peace of mind that accompanies a normal test. Interestingly, normal testing does not seem to ease their hearts because they do not have the type of faith outlined in Hebrews 11:1: "Now faith is being sure of what we hope for and certain of what we do not see."

Joanne's normal testing was helpful at defining her state of low risk eight years earlier, but no test guarantees you will never have a problem. We are on a journey of faith, trusting in Christ for our peace and strength.

We develop the ability to cope with anything when we learn how to lean into Christ. It is hard to know in our hearts how much God loves us and desires an intimate relationship with us, where we rely upon Him in everyday life.

For many, the fellowship with Jesus seems to take on less importance as the week begins and the stresses of life serve to distract. As Sunday comes and goes, we gain a false sense of control of our lives, which unfortunately causes our hearts to bear the burden of us fighting life's battles on our own strength.

We must understand that physical blessings are tied to spiritual blessings. Our efforts to achieve better physical lives are dependent upon what we are willing to invest in our spiritual relationships with God. We must put our trust and faith in our Lord to realize the benefits in our physical lives. It takes daily reading of God's Word to battle the lies of the Devil and to renew our minds with the truth of what He wants for us. We are encouraged in 1 Thessalonians 5:17 (NKJV) "to pray without ceasing," which literally means to fellowship with Him throughout the day. We are to have an attitude of constant fellowship. When we come to Him in this way, God shows His immense love for us and constant availability. He wants to teach us to trust Him even when there is little evidence of His presence in our lives.

Tied to the ER stretcher by IVs leading to bags of medications, the antiseptic smells of rubbing alcohol, the stings of the needles in her arms, and the rhythmic beat of the heart monitor overwhelming her senses, Joanne thought back to the time that she saw the cardiologist when she thought it was her heart eight years prior. It was easy for her to see the difference. The symptoms Joanne felt then were not at all similar to what she was now feeling. Joanne was now facing something she had never experienced before.

Once again, Joanne's experience is not intended to cause worry. Her risk for heart disease was very low, but no one has a *no-risk contract*. Uncommon things happen uncommonly. Joanne was not being punished. Nothing she did made this heart attack happen. Something happened, and we have to trust that God is in control. Adversity is one of God's tools to mold us into the person He wants and knows us to be. We all need pruning and molding, and only when we are frustrated and discontent with our current states can God come in and change us.

Hearing the doctors tell her she was having a heart attack did not seem real despite the evidence: the ECG, blood tests, and clinical presentation. What she had always worried about was now happening, and Joanne could not help but feel, in some ways, her worry and stress had brought it on herself. After all, why else would this be happening?

Throughout her life, Joanne knew that Jesus was Lord, but prayed with her mind and not her heart. She knew she was supposed to trust God, but in her own heart she felt that *God could only take you so far* and at some point *counseling was necessary* to help her overcome her issues with not being content. The heart attack had now caused worry and doubt to take over in light of her shaky foundation of God's love and power. She felt abandoned; she thought, *if God loved me, how could this happen to me?* In the midst of this trial, Joanne could not see how God wanted an intimate relationship with her in her daily life. The doubt was evident in the window of her eyes. She was finding it difficult to see how God's Word applied to her daily life. It was important now, more than ever, for Joanne to listen to the promises of God and to know that she was not only battling this heart attack, but the attack on her faith by the lies of the Devil. Faith is built on the study of the Word of God's promises. Our faith is pleasing to God. Admittedly, at this moment, it was hard for Joanne to understand that God uses our trials to get us to rely on Him more.

God was not putting Joanne through this to get her attention; however, through the heart attack, He could now get her to focus on Him and not her circumstances. In everything, give thanks, for this is the will of God for your life. His ways are not our ways. His thoughts are above our thoughts. Although it was difficult for Joanne to understand right now, whatever God does is good, and it does not matter what we feel about what God does. God does not guarantee us we will not face storms in life. In fact, He tells us there will be storms in our lives; however, He guarantees that He will always be with us through the storms. "I have told you these things, so that in me you may have peace. In this world you will have trouble. But take heart! I have overcome the world" (John 16:33).

At the time of the angiography, the branch of Joanne's back artery was closed, and the balloon and stent did more than restore blood flow to her physical heart. The instant the artery was opened, the immense chest discomfort that Joanne had been experiencing all afternoon immediately left her, and she whispered, "Thank you, Jesus." Joanne was beginning to see that no matter where you are, the Lord is with you wherever you go. He was certainly with her at this time when confronted with a heart attack that could have taken her life before she had ever really *done something with her life.* Joshua 1:9 reminds us, "Have I not commanded you? Be strong and courageous. Do not be terrified; do not be discouraged, for the LORD your God will be with you wherever you go." God promises in Hebrews 13:5 (NKJV), "Let your conduct be without covetousness; be content with what you have, because God has said, 'Never will I leave you; never will I forsake you.'" He has been with Joanne her entire life—at the time she was raising her kids as a stay-at-home mom, through the time that she was searching, through the time when she needed to start a career, and most importantly now during her heart attack. The bigger question is, are we with God wherever we go? Do we take Him with us through our highs and lows in life? What is certain is that He stands by His Word and is always with us.

We do not know God's plan for our lives. There is no explanation why Joanne suddenly had to endure a heart attack. What is certain, however, is that Joanne's example could help many like her, demonstrating this could happen to anyone and equally demonstrating the healing both physically and spiritually. Joanne now faced accepting the assignment of a strong and courageous witness to God's healing hand in our lives. "As water reflects a face, so a man's heart reflects the man" (Proverbs 27:19). Her witnessed physical healing will be obvious and will motivate those around her to make a stronger commitment to lifestyle changes. The fruit of her example will have a greater impact on the many who have been wandering, searching for something missing in their lives. A wandering spiritual heart problem actually affects many more people than heart disease which keeps us from enjoying God's daily blessings in our lives. Amazingly, the answer is before us all along in God's Word. "Let the peace of Christ rule in your hearts, since as members of one body you were called to peace. And be thankful" (Colossians 3:15).

Before her heart attack—from the world's perspectives—Joanne was on a path to success. From Joanne's perspective, she was searching for worldly things for success. From God's perspective, there was no peace, no fruit. She was busy with things that did not matter. She was not fruitful. The heart attack opened her eyes to see "How awesome is the LORD Most High, the great King over all the earth!" (Psalms 47:2) whose love is everlasting. She was more in pursuit of things and success to make her happy and fulfill her life, and not in pursuit of peace. Matthew 6:33 (NKJV) was the perfect solution to her searching: "But seek first the kingdom of God and His righteousness, and all these things shall be added to you."

Joanne was out of order, seeking things and not His peace. The heart attack showed her it was time to properly prioritize her life.

There was a time when Joanne could not see how you lived in conscious awareness of God's personal love and availability. She was now beginning to understand we have access to the anointing of the Holy Spirit—the Spirit of God—to live in our hearts so we can have peace. No one is perfect. That is why He gave us amazing grace that cannot be earned by achievements in life.

To have a peaceful heart takes total surrender to God's will, but this was not what I first saw when I evaluated the obstacles Joanne would have to overcome. This is how it can truly *be the heart*, even when it is not the physical heart. The physical heart will respond to a spiritual heart in distress. "A cheerful heart is good medicine, but a crushed spirit dries up the bones" (Proverbs 17:22). We must learn to think right and put on the mind of Christ and learn "…to be content whatever the circumstances … in any and every situation, whether well fed or hungry, whether living in plenty or in want" (Philippians 4:11–12). Cast out the source of doubt and remove confusion and disorder in your life, "For God is not a God of disorder but of peace…" (1 Corinthians 14:33). To do this, we must be obedient and detailed in the Word of God.

Paraphrasing Joshua in chapter 1, verses 7–8, God tells us to be strong and very courageous, obey the Word of God, meditate on God's Word day and night, and to not deviate from His Word. The irony in Joanne's presentation is that this time it was her physical heart after years of suffering with a spiritual heart problem. Because she had such a low risk of developing heart disease, there was no reason to fear, yet Joanne always worried she would die of a heart attack.

She was now beginning to see that when you pray in faith, you declare your needs to God. Anxiety represents the absence of faith. It took going through a physical heart problem to begin the process of healing her spiritual heart. She was now able to ask God to teach her to depend on Him and not her own ability to solve things for herself. We are all on a journey, and this journey is made easier when we fellowship with God daily. We are His workmanship. Commit your day to the Lord, and pray your way through the moments. This will result in the closeness of His presence. "The poor will see and be glad—you who seek God, may your hearts live!" (Psalms 69:32).

Chapter 5

Commitment

Commit your way to the Lord, Trust also in Him, And he shall bring it to pass.

—Psalm 37:5 (NKJV)

Thankfully, God occasionally sprinkles patients into my practice who are well on the path to recovery. They are usually secure in their relationship with Jesus, have committed their lives to following His Word, and—despite having a history of coronary artery disease—have worked to maintain good physical heart health. As a cardiologist, it is sometimes emotionally draining to render lifesaving and life-changing physical and spiritual heart counsel only to watch the counsel go largely ignored. Fortunately, God knows my frustrations and provides some balance to my practice by leading those patients to me who are unquestionably dedicated to good heart health.

You tend to get to know these people by name, and even before going into the exam room, you fully expect the answer to any question like "How are you doing?" to be a true reflection on God's joy in their lives. Jesus wants our lives to be like a lamp, and how we respond to physical illness says much about His Light shining in us. These patients, too, experience trials and troubles on earth, but know to whom they should turn for their daily support. In short, they come to the office once a year, need far fewer tests and procedures, and are a joy to behold thanks to their godly attitudes.

Jim Oliver is just such a joy-filled person. Jim is a sixty-three-year-old male who suffered a heart attack and subsequent open heart bypass surgery twelve years ago. Since that time, I have been seeing him on a yearly basis to monitor his heart health. Jim is committed to a physically healthy heart—exercising briskly at least forty-five minutes every day, and following a low-fat, low-cholesterol diet to minimize the potential for recurring heart blockages. Jim is nearly always smiling and appears much younger than his sixty-three years. Except for the scar in the middle of his chest—which is an everyday reminder that he does not ever want to endure another lifesaving procedure again—one would never know he had coronary disease. Jim is also exceptionally thoughtful. On the day of his annual office visit, he always comes in bearing a gift. On this visit, Jim presented me with a spiritually uplifting book.

To be sure, Jim—like all of us—had, and currently has, his fair share of weaknesses, but he is deeply rooted in the Lord and turns to Him for strength to make it through whatever trials and tribulations he may face in his life. In fact, Jim is a former smoker who—without pills, patches, or gum—had no problems putting cigarettes down, as God answered his prayers by taking the desire from him. The heart attack truly took Jim by complete surprise. He never thought of life as his responsibility to take care of his body through exercise and healthy food choices. At that time, with the diagnosis of heart disease, the primary question in his mind became, "Is this going to be a death sentence, or am I going to change my ways of living so I can live life to its fullest?" Jim will tell you that good habits take time to develop and changing is not easy. "After all," he often says, "I have been trying—albeit sometimes unsuccessfully—to walk down the pathway to positive change most of my adult life."

The important lesson Jim has learned is that good habits can be developed over time, the same way bad habits are developed. Then, before you know it, your newly acquired habits have become a part of what and who you are for as long as you can remember. Experience has taught me that the habit-forming nature of exercise is not only fueled by the endorphin release that provides a feeling of well-being, but also by the stress relief and time alone with God meditating on the events of the day. Developing a deeper relationship with God has allowed Jim to cope with the troubles of life's daily stresses. God promises to build His truth into our lives so our character and conduct reflect His presence. In Ephesians 6:12, God reminds us "For our struggle is not against flesh and blood, but against the rulers, against the authorities, against the powers of this dark world and against the spiritual forces of evil in the heavenly realms."

Because patients like Jim usually take good care of their bodies, it is not necessarily imperative that they be seen by me each year. However, the confidence it gives these patients to know that God has blessed them with someone to help guide them to the path of good heart health provides a welcome measure of reassurance to them. It seems these patients always feel better after seeing me in the office—perhaps in the same way it makes me feel better after listening to a good message from a good preacher. God's Word has power and life! The truth of the Word is naturally uplifting, which makes us feel good and filled with hope.

My visits with Jim in the office are refreshing, as we are both in agreement with the power of our Lord in our daily lives. He has committed himself to a long life of physical and spiritual growth, hoping his life will be a living witness for everyone to see His glory in him.

Patients like these in my practice provide me the reassurance of God's healing powers in their lives and remind me of how all things are possible with Him in our hearts. In so many ways, these patients are as beneficial to me as they feel I am to them.

Just as it takes time and effort to invest in relationships with our wives, kids, families, and good friends to enjoy the fruit of this harvest, it is also necessary to have the type of relationship with God that He desires. God wants our spiritual hearts, the center of our lives ever after. He wants us to grow stronger spiritual hearts through the study of His Word; it requires a commitment of time and effort to develop this relationship with our Lord and Savior. Changes in our hearts change the way we speak, and like Christ, we can communicate God's forgiveness and love. "… For out of the overflow of his heart his mouth speaks" (Luke 6:45). Jesus gave His life for us so that we may live more abundantly. It is difficult for us humans to wrap our minds around the most central of Christian concepts of knowing how much He loves us. The development of a strong, caring, spiritual heart takes time, commitment, and focused effort. We cannot expect to grow a strong spiritual heart without cultivation and commitment. God instructs us to keep His commands in our hearts. "My son, do not forget my teaching, but keep my commands in your heart, for they will prolong your life many years and bring you prosperity" (Prov. 3:1–2). The same commitment of time and effort are needed to develop strong, healthy physical hearts. *I may not feel like jogging today, but I'm going anyway. It may be tempting to eat fast food today, but I will opt for a healthy meal at home instead.* Truthfully, I do not often feel like exercising and eating healthy … but I do it anyway. I try to remind myself that it is not how I *feel* that's important when it comes time to do the right things regarding taking care of God's temple. Nonverbal communication is as important as verbal communication. How do your actions speak?

If you are not speaking and are being observed, how strong is your witness for Christ? In a casual and non-guilt-imposing manner, I often ask patients who continually make excuses for their lack of diet and exercise discipline, "So, how do you think God sees our unwillingness to eat right and exercise as He watches us from heaven?"

People who do not exercise often characterize those who do exercise as having it easy. They do not realize that the aches and pains of feet, ankles, knees, hips, and body simply *go with the territory* of commitment to exercise. This particularly resonated from a personal understanding when I heard Mr. Oliver describe that he had discomfort with each step when he started to exercise each day. Amazingly, by the end of his four miles, communion with God had distracted him from noticing this discomfort, and he triumphantly finished his daily routine faster and with more vigor than when he started. Now that Jim is closer to retirement, he finds himself with considerably more time on his hands. Without the daily time constraints of a busy work schedule, Jim finds it easier to exercise when he is able to pick the best time of the day for his body to withstand the rigors of his workout. We laughed in agreement at how easy it is to exercise on beautiful, warm days rather than cold, gray, rainy days. We also know that our commitments to maintaining our bodies must remain unwavering, rain or shine. Commitment is mental but runs counter to our rebellious nature. God wants our minds to be committed. He reminds us in Romans 12:2, "Do not conform any longer to the pattern of this world, but be transformed by the renewing of your mind. Then you will be able to test and approve what God's will is—his good, pleasing and perfect will."

One of my favorite psalms serves as constant encouragement that we all need to pursue a righteous way of life. "Blessed is the man who does not walk in the counsel of the wicked or stand in the way of sinners or sit in the seat of mockers. But his delight is in the law of the LORD, and on his law he meditates day and night. He is like a tree planted by streams of water, which yields its fruit in season and whose leaf does not wither. Whatever he does prospers" (Psalms 1:1–3). Acknowledging the need to exercise—along with a deep planting of the seeds of good spiritual habits—helps us succeed at our commitments to our overall physical and spiritual health, even when we do not necessarily *feel like it*. Prior to his heart attack and bypass surgery, Jim had adopted an "I really and truly don't have time to exercise" mentality. Yet in reality—like so many of us who have a PhD in alibis—he had adopted a heart and mind full of excuses.

Jim needed to renew his mind in order to renew his heart.

There were parallel changes in Jim's daily life as a result of his change of heart. God does not limit His healing powers to one area of our lives. Psalm 19:14, "May the words of my mouth and the meditation of my heart be pleasing in your sight, O LORD, my Rock and my Redeemer" is applicable to everything in our lives. Jim was always a devoted and caring husband and father, but his new change of heart resulted in the bearing of better and healthier fruit in this area of his life as well. Leading by example also helped him sow seeds for a healthier, happier life for his family. As the founder of a small technology company that has now become a formidable business entity, Jim has been fortunate to experience a transformation from comfortably supporting his family to the success of having abundance.

This abundance has allowed him to work less and spend more time with the loved ones he holds closest to his heart. He has even been able to give control of the day-to-day operations to his son and focus more as a consultant. God has truly blessed him—even to the extent of providing him with more time to care for his body. Since his heart attack, Jim has built steadily on his life-changing commitment to not only a healthy physical heart, but a healthy spiritual one as well. In both cases, evidence clearly points to the rejuvenating powers of exercising his heart and his mind.

In Jim's most recent office visit, as a part of his routine screening, it was time for him to take a walk on the treadmill. Just as I expected, his treadmill time confirmed that his daily exercise regimen, coupled with a heart-healthy diet, yielded outstanding test results. Jim is striving hard to prevent the progression of his heart blockages, and his hard work is paying off.

Actually it is easy to maintain physical heart health when you first make the commitment to spiritual heart health. Jim completed stage IV of the standard treadmill and was actually stopped by the technician, even though he could have walked much farther. This simple ten-minute exercise alone served as a good indicator in conveying Jim's overall low risk for a cardiac event.

Jim's commitment to a healthy diet is also a good indicator of his continued good health. As noted earlier, he certainly appears younger than his stated age and has a robust color and is physically fit in every sense of the word. Admittedly, Jim has been more strictly adhering to his diet since the heart attack and has nearly lost the temptation to indulge in unhealthy, fatty foods.

Yolande, Jim's wife, has continued to be—as Jim calls it—his "food watchdog." Her active involvement in helping Jim subscribe to nutritious life choices has contributed greatly to his fitness. Similarly, I shared with Jim how my wife Mary's lunches for our children were legendary throughout high school. Even in the face of fast-food snacks that littered the lives of their peers, the Constantine kids' sandwiches, fruit, nuts—and water—were the envy of their friends. In the same manner, Yolande has learned to take the time to prepare nutritious meals for Jim and the kids, before they left to live lives of their own. This selfless giving by wives helps set the foundation by all to actively take personal responsibility for the things we feed our bodies. There are always going to be times of straying from what is best, but God knows our hearts and rewards us for the pattern of our behavior——the body of work.

Of course, there are still times when Jim experiences chest discomfort, pain, pressure, palpitations, skips in his heartbeat, shortness of breath, fatigue—and even an occasional lightheaded spell when he momentarily wonders, *Is it my heart?* But it does not take Jim long to quickly recover from this momentary fear by standing firmly on his commitment to his faith, with his eyes focused only upon God's love and truth.

Jim knows that he will receive God's reward of good heart health because of offering his body to God. In Romans 6:11–14, God tells us, "In the same way, count yourselves dead to sin but alive to God in Christ Jesus. Therefore do not let sin reign in your mortal body so that you obey its evil desires. Do not offer the parts of your body to sin, as instruments of wickedness, but rather offer yourselves to God, as those who have been brought from death to life; and offer the parts of your body to him as instruments of righteousness. For sin shall not be your master, because you are not under law, but under grace."

God wants a living sacrifice. It is our relationships with Christ that put the living in sacrifice.

The office visits with Jim, and patients like him, serve to confirm our positions in God's army. It also reaffirms our need to take care of our bodies and live our lives in a manner that would bring glory to God. It is only natural for heart patients who have survived a heart attack to worry—sometimes excessively—over the possibility of having another one. With Jim, however, there is no worry. With faith, he will continue to commit to a healthy lifestyle and will assuredly receive God's blessings and good health. Jim's personal peace comes through his communion with God in prayer, as directed in Philippians 4:6–7: "Do not be anxious about anything, but in every thing, by prayer and petition, with thanksgiving, present your requests to God. And the peace of God, which transcends all understanding, will guard your hearts and your minds in Christ Jesus." Jim's physical heart—and body—has changed, but it could not have happened without first changing his spiritual heart. Yet the very essence of this story of Jim's transition to a stronger heart is not one of simply change, but rather, of the underlying commitment to change. Jesus gave him the strength and wisdom when he was down, but Jim had to take the first step to commit to drawing near to God to receive His blessings in his life.

"For the eyes of the LORD range throughout the earth to strengthen those whose hearts are fully committed to him…" (2 Chron. 16:9). As contradictory as it sounds, something as bad as a heart attack—which could have literally killed Jim—actually helped him to live. Our God truly works in mysterious ways, doesn't He?

Chapter 6

Faith—Unaware

But without faith it is impossible to please Him, for he who comes to God must believe that He is, and that He is a rewarder of those who diligently seek Him.

—Hebrews 11:6 (NKJV)

Some things never change, I thought to myself as I walked into the exam room and was greeted by fifty-three-year-old Leroy Harris, looking almost exactly as unhealthy as he first appeared to me eight months previous while suffering from a heart attack that nearly took his life.

My first thought was one of utter disbelief, imagining how I could have been on the same interstate with this very unhealthy man with his big rig bearing down closely on the rear bumper of my car. I could almost visualize in my rearview mirror the nauseating sight of chewing tobacco dripping down the corner of his mouth as I tried to steady my car down the interstate. *Wow, I thought, what if he had a heart attack at that moment?*

Here stood Leroy Harris, a mountain of a man. At 347 pounds, the buttons on his grease-stained blue Stevens Trucking shirt were one thread from bursting open to reveal his undershirt. His suspenders were stretched to the max trying to keep his dark blue uniform pants from being what teenagers call fashionable lowriders. His unshaven face and unkempt hair gave me the impression Leroy had pulled his truck into the hospital parking lot after returning to Nashville from an all-night drive from Anywhere USA without first going home to shower, which—given his appearance—was likely the case. I am sure the disappointment was evident in my eyes. Over eight months had passed since his brush with near death. It was hard to understand how Leroy had veered so close to the guardrail of life's highway that sparks flew from his truck, and yet he had done almost nothing to change his destructive course.

He, of course, had many excuses, but no honest reasons. Before I even had the chance to ask how things were going, Leroy looked away almost apologetically and began telling me that because he was on the road a lot, he "didn't have the time to exercise or eat right or any of that other stuff I'm supposed to be doin'"—as if he had no control over his life.

Leroy's visit reminded me that we are all on the same road of life. From birth to death, I like to call it *I-65 north to heaven*. God reveals to each of us the specific path we should follow. However, it takes us studying His Word and having a relationship with our Lord for this path to be revealed to our hearts. Despite Satan's lies to try to convince us we are victims and cannot change our courses to enjoy the bounties God wants for us, the truth is that Christ came to set us free, to empower us to overcome life's obstacles with Him as our guide. There are many diversions and so-called shortcuts along the way to the Way, but these only serve to distract us and get us lost from the true path of peace for our lives. There are times in everyone's life when we are tempted to take an exit that sidetracks us from the purpose He has for our lives. It takes faith and perseverance and constant fellowship with God to stay focused and get back on the path that leads us to victory. When times are difficult, it takes faith to know His truth. But in the end, our faithfulness will be rewarded with the blessings He has promised us.

Being faithful is necessary to break the stronghold the Enemy has over us. Do what is right when no one else is, even if it doesn't feel right or doesn't look like we are getting the right results fast enough to suit us. It is not about us, but what He can do through us for His glory. We are born with everything we need to be a spiritually health person, but we have to exercise it to get it to show. The same principles apply to a healthy physical heart; exercise is not an option, but a necessity.

Strength in spirit sustains us in times of bodily pain, injury, or suffering. This is a principle Leroy would have to learn and practice to enjoy the spoils of a long, healthy physical life on earth and life everlasting in heaven.

God does not favor one person over another, one job over another, or one race or nationality over another. He loves us all the same and wants the best for each of us. To receive the blessings of a healthy life requires hard work. God tells us to be faithful over little; He will make us rulers over much. Time will reveal our harvests of good health, and it is important to stay focused on God's encouraging Word, rather than Satan's lies, to remain diligent, persistent, and fruitful in our journeys. Borrowing from Leroy's terms, the journey to good health is a *long-haul road trip.*

"But the seed on good soil stands for those with a noble and good heart, who hear the word, retain it, and by persevering produce a crop" (Luke 8:15).

Leroy's severe heart issues besieged him eight months earlier as he was returning from just one of these road trips, driving all night to return from Baton Rouge, Louisiana, where he stopped to unload and pick up another trailer full of freight on his way back from California. A week ago, he left Murfreesboro, Tennessee, with a full truck headed for San Diego, California, with his wife, Annette—his trip companion and designated relief driver when he got too tired. Over two thousand miles and three days later, they pulled into a San Diego warehouse. After unloading his rig—which I can only describe as a purple and gold Fire Dragon—he reloaded for Baton Rouge, where he would go through the same routine of unloading and reloading for the trip back to Nashville.

In a life *very out of balance,* this routine repeated itself throughout the year, year after year, with very little time at home. For Leroy, however, being behind the wheel of the big rig the majority of the time was like being at home. Annette would usually give him a six-hour break at midnight while he attempted to grab a few winks in the sleeper cab of the truck. They stopped to refuel, regroup, and eat at truck stops—which is not exactly an oasis of nutrition catering to a healthy lifestyle. Leroy and Annette were not alone. There were many drivers with various degrees of similarity on the road. They did not waste much time, as *time was money* to Leroy; the longer it took him to get home, the fewer trips he could make. He was emphatic in letting me know that he "wasn't getting any younger" and didn't know how long he "could keep up this pace."

"How in the heck would I make a livin' then, Doc?" he asked. As I have outlined in other chapters, Leroy and Annette had a laundry list of *reasons* why it was *impossible* to exercise or eat right on the road. The real reason—appearing nowhere on their list—was the unavoidable fact that taking care of their body-temples was not a priority. Without reluctance, they admitted believing in God, but didn't take time to know Him or have the time to read His Word to know the truth about His plan for them. Leroy staunchly claimed that he didn't have the time to worry about his health because he was too busy trying to stay awake. No doubt, the steady stream of caffeine, nicotine, chewing tobacco, and other stimulants helped him keep his *focus* on the road, but not on the Lord.

This particular trip felt different to Leroy. He was noticing more shortness of breath and fatigue while loading barrels of chemicals on and off his truck than he ever did before. Oh, to be sure, he was always winded—his massive size of 347 pounds, smoking two to three packs per day, and lack of exercise assured this.

In Baton Rouge, the shortness of breath became so unbearable that Leroy felt like he "couldn't go on," which he had never felt before. He even began to experience a heaviness, as he called it, in his chest. "It must have been those country-fried steaks [yes, steaks, plural] I had for dinner last night," he told himself. But belching did not relieve what he thought was gas. Annette was becoming more concerned with each passing mile marker. She knew something was seriously wrong with Leroy when he freely let her drive the rig most of the journey back to Nashville, something he rarely ever allowed. Leroy felt better after resting for most of the night and early morning and was manning the wheel at 5:00 a.m. Suddenly, sweat began to pour out onto his head, with the fullness in his chest now recurring and causing him to feel as though he were "going to explode." He began to experience dizziness so extreme he was certain that he was going to pass out at any moment. Annette helped Leroy wrestle the big rig over to the side of the interstate, where she frantically called 911 to have paramedics meet them to rush Leroy to the emergency room. Her instincts told her that it wasn't reflux making him *look like a dying man.*

In the ER, the ECG revealed the reality that he was having a heart attack. Drenched in sweat, pale, and clammy, Leroy remembered fading in and out and remembered little about the experience except his hearing the beep of the heart monitor, which let him know he was still alive. Since the heart is so important to life, each passing moment of damage to heart muscle becomes increasingly critical. It is extremely important to open the offending heart artery with a balloon or stent as quickly as possible to save heart muscle and to experience significantly better outcomes.

Leroy went from the emergency-room door to the cardiac cath-lab table, where an arteriogram and balloon and stent rescued him—literally within minutes—from the assault on his physical heart.

It is amazing how things are not always as they seem. Just like those patients who should not have heart problems sometimes do, those with the most risk factors for heart disease do not necessarily have the worst coronary artery disease. Even the patients who take the least care of their hearts sometimes have overall less severe heart disease. As a testament to God's watching over us even when we don't watch over ourselves, Leroy's heart arteries were much better than one would have predicted by his outward appearance. With the exception of the 100 percent blockage in the right coronary artery, which was causing his heart attack, Leroy's other arteries were large, fittingly to supply his large body, and there was only mild evidence of cholesterol lining his heart arteries.

In a cath-lab moment like Leroy's, opening the heart artery can, at times (and did in Leroy's case), cause electrical problems that make things worse before getting better. Much like other trials we endure in life, it seems that oftentimes things are darkest before dawn. Despite being sedated, Leroy recalled feeling peace with the relief of his heart attack. As is nearly always the case, lasting peace would be harder for Leroy to achieve and would come from the hard work of changing his life. Over the course of the next few weeks, Leroy would begin feeling better and find himself well on the road to physical heart recovery.

God may have led Leroy to a procedure to save his life, but Leroy would have to ultimately change his life—a much more difficult task than anyone ever expects. It would take faith in our Lord Jesus for Leroy to achieve victory over the obstacles that stood in the way of real change. Like David of the Old Testament, it would take faith in God's Word to slay a seemingly overpowering Goliath in his life. Smoking, obesity, horrible nutrition, lack of exercise, and no discipline were *giants* that will overtake Leroy without God's strength and guidance in his life.

In Psalm 18:1–3, David tells us, "I love you, O LORD, my strength. The LORD is my rock, my fortress and my deliverer; my God is my rock, in whom I take refuge. He is my shield and the horn of my salvation, my stronghold. I call to the LORD, who is worthy of praise, and I am saved from my enemies."

Little by little God shows us how the more we trust, the more progress we make. God will not do our parts, and we cannot do His part. We do what we can do, and He does what we cannot do. To change his life, Leroy would have to not only accept, but also wholeheartedly embrace, change. His whole focus would have to change, and for the first time in his life, Leroy would have to make his body a priority. Change would take time, whatever the problem, and in his case, there were many problems. We think we have to *run* and do everything at once when we first need to *rest* in the Word of God. God gives us a wonderful assurance of this in Matthew 11:28: "Come to me, all you who are weary and burdened, and I will give you rest." And we have to read His Word—which is our manual on life—to learn what He wants for our lives before jumping into action. The Bible restores you to your rightful position. It points out where we are weak and how to be strong. It points out where we are sick and how to get well. It points out where we are dirty and how to get clean. The Bible instructs, rebukes, corrects, and trains. The Bible is God's GPS—God's Plan of Salvation. It helps us get right and stay right. God does things satellites can't do. He tells us when we are lost before we know it and guides us on how to get to heaven.

There are no quick fixes. Like David, we need to trust God to overcome our giants. We will not experience physical and spiritual wellness in an instant. We should not get discouraged in the face of our sinful nature. Even David—a man after God's own heart—had many sins.

Constant prayer is needed to fellowship with Him and strengthen us in our weaknesses and keep us protected from the Enemy's attack.

There is an *amazing parallel in physical and spiritual heart healing*, and I believe we have to exercise both before achieving the ultimate in heart health. You cannot get in optimal physical heart health until you address the regimen necessary to achieve spiritual heart health. As incredible as it sounds, many people experience a life-threatening event, endure an invasive lifesaving procedure, and yet go home and act as though they want to repeat the same life-threatening process all over again. Without getting our hearts right, knowing how to battle the Devil's attack becomes so overwhelming in our minds that we make only a token effort to give the healing process over to God in order to reap the harvest of good physical heart health. The scriptural truth behind this rests upon Matthew 19:26: "Jesus looked at them and said, 'With man this is impossible, but with God all things are possible.'"

After nearly dying at an age *too young to die*, Leroy had come back into the office, by his report, feeling "pretty fair." He was no longer having any variation of chest pain, chest pressure, chest discomfort, chest fullness, or heaviness. He was now content with his *normal* shortness of breath that he had had for as long as he could remember. Upon entering the exam room, it did not require a cardiologist to see the evidence of what Leroy was not doing to stay off the highway to another heart attack. I think he was surprised that I did not "jump all over him" like he complained Annette had been doing in light of his obviously ignoring those things necessary to avoid another heart attack.

Utilizing the unique platform God has given me to teach the good news of what the Lord has for our lives, I attempted to help Leroy focus on heart healing from the standpoint of understanding the truth in order for him to begin the long trip toward freedom from his *giants*. I encouraged him to make up his mind to not let these giants beat him. He needed to know in his heart that he did not have to give up his future because of his past. I truly felt as though he wanted to know the wonderful feeling of being able to experience whole-heart healing, both physical and spiritual. Jesus came to heal the broken heart. We must be confident in who we are in Christ so we will not be subject to our giants. Shortly thereafter, and amazingly, Leroy stopped smoking two to three packs per day. However, he unfortunately significantly increased his amount of chewing tobacco per day—justifying it by claiming "this was the only way he could stop smoking." Of even greater misfortune, after a brief time in cardiac rehabilitation, Leroy simply refused to continue trying to heal his heart, no longer making the effort to utilize the structure, guidance, and encouragement cardiac rehab provided.

As hard as it was to imagine, he actually gained five pounds on his frame that was already too big for a heavyweight wrestler. He continued to travel across country as often as he had before because, he said, "too many people depend on me" and "I need the money." He had not changed any of his eating habits, lamenting that he could not find a healthy place to eat because they wouldn't allow him to pull his big rig into their parking lot. Leroy had not gotten the exercise and rest his body needed for renewing, stating almost defiantly, "You just don't know how difficult this is to do with my job." For most areas of life that Leroy needed to change, he was sadly content to believe the lies of the Devil as truth. Leroy was an easy mark for deception since he had spent absolutely no time studying God's Word to know the truth of what God says about him. Leroy knows the problems facing him and even knows what it is like to be dying from a heart attack, but he needs to hear how it is possible with God's help to change his heart and *move his truck* (body) *to a lower-risk road*—words that he has not heard before. The world has convinced Leroy that change is too hard and not worth the effort.

Therefore, his time in my office was best spent opening the eyes of his heart to the truth. I have spent considerable time encouraging him to know "everything is possible through Christ" is not just a conveniently quoted verse from Scripture.

Never deny the power of God's promises. God's Word contains promises for situations precisely like the ones Leroy is facing. Leroy cannot run away from his problems. He will run into the problems at some point in his life, and God will ultimately force him—like all of us—to deal with the issues before going forward. We can walk away from a problem—sweep it aside—but the problem never goes away. It is left in your soul. The problem becomes a part of you until you finally deal with the issue. Hebrews 10:35–36 presents a great lesson in perseverance: "So do not throw away your confidence; it will be richly rewarded. You need to persevere so that when you have done the will of God, you will receive what He has promised."

Leroy was trying to deal with his issues with his own strength. The path of least resistance was easiest. It was easier continuing on his unhealthy path of not changing. I can only give him the formula to change, but the implementing of the plan for personal success will fall on the heart of Leroy. God warns us there will be distracters—and in Leroy's life, there were many to try to discourage him when he no longer lived like those around him lived. God instructs us to run the good race and in many ways tells us it is not a sprint, but—like Leroy's job—a long-haul journey, a marathon. We have to keep focused on the prize that will be ours when we run to win. People try to run with Christ before first learning to sit and listen to Him. Even when people are told by God what they must do to change, they are unable to take steps in that direction until first learning to rest in Him. Who is Jesus in your life?

We must answer this question first before we are able to deal with the stuff in our lives. We must seek wisdom. The Bible is our source of wisdom. Wisdom enables us to face trials with pure joy. "If any of you lacks wisdom, he should ask God, who gives generously to all without finding fault, and it will be given to him" (James 1:5). God also proclaims in Proverbs 3:13: "Blessed is the man who finds wisdom, the man who gains understanding." He also reminds us in Proverbs 4:7 that "Wisdom is supreme; therefore get wisdom. Though it cost all you have, get understanding." In Proverbs 8:11, He tells us "for wisdom is more precious than rubies, and nothing you desire can compare with her." When Leroy makes wise choices regarding his health, good results will follow. Time will reveal his harvest of good health. Humanity looks at our outward appearances, but God always looks at our hearts. When God captures your heart, you will capture His will for your life—and to God, no harvest could be any more sweet or bountiful.

Chapter 7

Teaching Us to Trust

'You will seek me and find me when you seek me with all your heart."

—Jeremiah 29:13

It isn't uncommon for someone to cry out, "Why me, God?" when diagnosed with a severe health problem. But a more accurate response from all of us to the onset of any disease would be, "Why not me, God?" Disease does not discriminate. Depending on the type and timing, disease has a predictable way of creeping into the lives of all of us. When it comes to heart disease, I have seen it in every type of man and woman imaginable. It does not matter how old you are or where you went to school (or didn't), or how much money you have, or on which side of the tracks you find yourself living. Disease does not care whether you check Caucasian, African American, Hispanic, Asian, or Other on your census form. Occupations provide no barrier to disease either; doctors, presidents, and ministers are just as likely to face disease as construction workers, garbage collectors, or farmers.

God never promised us disease would not strike. He simply promised He would always be with us, no matter what trials we might have to endure. In Isaiah 53:5, He tells us, "But he was pierced for our transgressions, he was crushed for our iniquities; the punishment that brought us peace was upon him, and by his wounds we are healed." Trials are God's way of testing and teaching. He tests our faith in His ability to help us overcome, and He teaches us to trust in His strength, not our own. Some of the godliest men and women I know and treat from all walks of life—including ministers—have battled heart disease.

Although I have several ministers who depend on me to heal their hearts of various physical ailments, very few of them feel as though they are in need of ministering to their spiritual hearts—after all, this is *their specialty.* Pastor Jeremiah (as I'll call him) was no different when I first met him over sixteen years ago. At that time, he was a stout, fifty-nine-year-old, robust African American man, five feet nine inches tall and weighing 245 pounds, with thick forearms that made him look more like a sawmill operator—or maybe a middle linebacker—than a minister. His infectious personality filled up any room he entered. When he smiled, you smiled ... and when he spoke, you listened.

As a preacher of the gospel, Pastor Jeremiah boldly led revivals to listeners throughout small towns in rural Tennessee, inviting and encouraging people to experience the love of Jesus. It was during one of these revivals on a hot, steamy August night that Pastor Jeremiah broke out in profuse sweat that he had experienced countless times before. Yet something about this episode was different. This was not a routine sweat from the heat of the moment or the night, but rather, as he described it, an "intense cold sweat"—like a cool drenching rain, followed by a dull aching sensation like he'd never felt before.

"The harder I preached," he explained in his big, booming voice, "the harder it was for me to breathe." While many people recall the sensation of a heart attack as an elephant sitting on their chest, Pastor Jeremiah gestured with his huge arms wrapped around his upper body and described it through a clinched-teeth grimace as "the Devil trying his best to squeeze the very breath out of my chest to shut me up from preaching the salvation of Christ!"

Amid a chorus of *amens* from the crowd, the excruciating chest pressure worsened and resulted in the passionate preacher's knees suddenly buckling, causing him to collapse in the pulpit.

To Pastor Jeremiah, the remainder of that sultry summer night was a blur of a speeding ambulance ride, a screaming siren, emergency medical personnel, IVs and heart monitors, and worried family and friends. He quickly found himself going from the heat of the night to the air-conditioned cold of the cardiac catheterization lab. Vaguely, he recalled the discussion about the results of the coronary arteriography.

"Pastor, we've found severe blockages in the arteries in your heart," his cardiologist (a young Dr. Constantine) stated, "which unfortunately will require the surgeon to perform open-heart bypass surgery on you immediately."

As suddenly as the heart attack had overtaken him in the pulpit, Pastor Jeremiah found himself faced with the decision for bypass surgery equally as suddenly. "There wasn't even any time for me to worry," he later laughed. "All I could do was pray while they wheeled me into the operating room."

The only things that passed more quickly than the operation and recovery were the ensuing sixteen years that I have been seeing Pastor Jeremiah in the office.

In spite of the pain and drama that fueled the pastor's brush with a potentially fatal heart attack and subsequent surgery that involved the splitting of his chest, it was almost as if—at least in his mind—the bypass operation had never happened. He quickly resumed his ministry schedule at the same stressful, seven-day-a-week pace as before the bypass operation. His life's work once again consumed his entire life, but—like many heart patients whose lives have been spared through coronary bypass—Pastor Jeremiah, unfortunately, never really took time to modify his lifestyle to prevent heart disease from recurring. Although his physical heart was healed with the open-heart surgery, Pastor Jeremiah never *practiced what he preached* by addressing his spiritual heart needs.

In many ways, he was trusting God for healing but never put forth the effort to claim this healing. As far as biblical fundamentals go, the pastor did not smoke or drink. I seriously doubt he ever used profane language. I'm absolutely certain he had a godly heart to care for others and to spread the Word. However, Pastor Jeremiah was not truly living the life Jesus had for him. He was an addict—but not chemically addicted in the classic sense. His addiction, like that of so many people in the country today, was lack of discipline in making proper food choices and exercising his body. Webster defines *lazy* as adverse or disinclined to activity. It was not that the pastor felt that it wasn't necessary to alter his diet or to take time each day and exercise the temple God had given him. In his words, diet and exercise discipline were weaknesses in his life that he always had trouble controlling.

The pastor playfully shifted the blame to Mrs. Jeremiah, who continued to prepare meals that were no doubt delicious, but also rich in everything from which a heart patient should logically refrain. However, the real blame rested squarely upon the broad shoulders of the pastor, who simply refused to eat sensible portions. His lack of exercise was attributed to the weather, the time demands of his job, or the catchall statement of blame associated with arthritis, which affected all of the joints of his large body.

Mrs. Jeremiah would always accompany her husband to the office for his yearly checkups, and each visit would be a wonderful mixture of not only monitoring his heart disease, blood pressure, cholesterol, and overall health, but also learning more about his recent revivals.

We would always talk about their five children and numerous grandchildren, with he and I agreeing on how family confirms the goodness and blessings of almighty God in all our lives. But when it came time to talk seriously about the obstacles to prevent his recurring heart disease, Pastor Jeremiah would become uncharacteristically quiet. On a couple of visits, he joked about his inability to lose his stomach and control his weight because of Mrs. Jeremiah's "feeding me too well." On the one hand, he openly admitted to the need to lose weight, while on the other hand, he seemed reluctant to ask God to help him with this personal struggle. Here was a man, I thought, whose counsel with others would nearly always be punctuated with strong advice to *turn it over to the Lord*, as in Psalm 37:5 (NKJV): "Commit your way to the Lord, Trust also in Him, And He shall bring it to pass." Yet somehow he could not bring himself to heed the same advice. God teaches us to trust in His strength, not our own.

Actually, Pastor Jeremiah considered himself as doing okay. After all, it had been more than sixteen years since his bypass operation. The surgeon who performed his bypass told him there was a possibility he might develop new blockages in ten to fifteen years. So in the pastor's mind, he had already beaten the odds. But the Devil's objective is to trick us into believing a lie as the truth. He is intent upon convincing us to give up—and he will stop at nothing to accomplish this goal. Although Pastor Jeremiah did not admit to giving up, the Devil provided him with a head full of excuses to keep him from fully enjoying the healthy life God had for him. It was all too easy to fall back on his hectic schedule of doing God's work as an excuse to ignore the lifesaving lifestyle changes of diet and exercise in order to keep his heart healthy.

Just as the blockages in his arteries prevented blood from flowing to his heart muscle at the time of his heart attack, there were blockages to the pastor's spiritual heart that prevented God's blessings from flowing through his life.

In the early years after bypass surgery, Pastor Jeremiah had come to know and trust me to guide him with godly counsel regarding the path to take to monitor his heart health. Physically, until now, Pastor Jeremiah was seemingly doing well. However, just as physicians need doctors, ministers need someone to minister to their heart, too. They are not immune to the attacks of the Devil. These lies from the Enemy made it okay for him to immerse himself in his job and not take the time to exercise daily and make healthier food choices. Although knowing the truth in his heart about what God said about him, it was difficult for him to resist the Devil's lies when it came time to change his life. Even when I would share stories of how many of my patients tell me that my heart-health ministering would make me a great minister, this did not seem to resonate with Pastor Jeremiah. The Devil was attacking the pastor's mind, making him think the difficulties of a busy ministry, physical ailments, and a touch of arthritis and obesity, were insurmountable roadblocks to improving his overall health and heart health.

Each year his question, "How is my heart doing?" was fairly straightforwardly answered; appropriate and timely testing and yearly clinical evaluation confirmed the pastor's physical heart, despite not being fully taken care of, was doing well. In the office, his blood pressure was always elevated because of *white-coat syndrome* (even though I don't wear a white coat in my daily practice). With each visit, it became crystal clear that—although there was a time when Pastor Jeremiah needed physical heart healing—he now needed someone to minister to his spiritual heart health.

Many years ago, God revealed to me the *inseparable binding* of the spiritual and physical hearts. What we know God says about us from His Word makes it easier to stay motivated to take care of our physical hearts. Through the teachings about the heart, God showed me where poor spiritual heart health gets in the way of fully receiving the blessings of a long, healthy physical life. "Do you not know that your body is a temple of the Holy Spirit, who is in you, whom you have received from God? You are not your own; you were bought at a price. Therefore honor God with your body" (1 Corinthians 6:19–20). This command from 1 Corinthians is perhaps the most often quoted Scripture where God's Word actually commands us to care for our temples. No doubt, Pastor Jeremiah knew this Scripture as well as any he had ever studied. He also knew it in much the same way a smoker knows smoking is bad for his heart, lungs, and overall health. On a typical Sunday, I'm certain he preached about this very Scripture, yet when Monday rolled around, it was a message that did not penetrate his own heart.

In order to be a more effective witness and lead others to Christ, Pastor Jeremiah needed to lead by example and ask God's guidance in overcoming his addictions. I knew, however, that Pastor Jeremiah was a strong-willed man; I recognized that the door to this issue was closed at this time. I was confident there would be a time—God's time—when the pastor's heart would be receptive to change and the ultimate healing power of Jesus. Throughout the book of James, we are reminded that we are to maintain receptive hearts in order to be made complete in the eyes of God. God assures us in Jeremiah 30:17: "'But I will restore you to health and heal your wounds,' declares the LORD…"

It had been sixteen years since Pastor Jeremiah's open-heart surgery and ironically three months after seeing him in the office that a call came from Pastor Jeremiah's son, a family practice physician in a small mountainous town in Southeast Tennessee. He informed me his father had been admitted to a Knoxville hospital with a stroke. It happened on the night of a revival, much like the evening of his heart attack sixteen years earlier. According to his son, the pastor just didn't know where he was and was confused. This man whose sermons flowed from his mouth like water from a fountain suddenly found himself mentally disoriented and unable to utter even the simplest of words. *My God*, he thought, *something is terribly wrong.*

Miles away from home, he was taken to the nearest hospital in the Knoxville area. The family was understandably worried after hearing the word *stroke*. Although grounded in a lifetime of trust in their faith, everyone was admittedly thinking the worst. Pastor Jeremiah's son recommended the transfer of his father to familiar and comforting surroundings in Nashville, and I concurred. Despite this not being a true cardiac problem, transfer was arranged so I could care for my patient. Not knowing what to expect because of the family's panic about Pastor Jeremiah's stroke, I was pleasantly surprised that there was very little physical impairment from what turned out to be a mild stroke. The fear and emotional damage seen in Pastor Jeremiah and his family were far more significant than the physical impairment that he suffered from the stroke. Even though it was quite obvious the pastor had experienced God's physical blessings of rapid and probable complete healing from this stroke in such a short period of time, there was an unusual loss of faith and even confusion about where to turn by the pastor and his family.

When cardiac monitoring uncovered the presence of an irregular heart rhythm that was partially responsible for his stroke, Pastor Jeremiah's eyes were filled with worry. The physical and spiritual dimensions of the pastor's heart were completely out of sync, just like his physical heart rhythm.

This *fixable problem* opened a wound and left Pastor Jeremiah vulnerable to attack by the spirit of worry. Now, in addition to the stroke, his pathway to a full recovery was made more difficult by his fixating on *having another heart problem, too*. His worry and frustration turned into anger at himself as he experienced guilt, knowing that if sixteen years earlier, he had taken better care of himself after open-heart surgery, this current problem may not have happened.

In spite of the most recent problem, the preacher's physical heart was in better shape now than sixteen years ago at the time of his emergency operation, but spiritually his heart was critically ill. The pastor forgot that trials were God's way of testing our faith in His ability while teaching us to trust in His strength, not our own. Moreover, he had forgotten the lesson in perseverance found in 1 Corinthians, 9:24–25: "Do you not know that in a race all the runners run, but only one gets the prize? Run in such a way as to get the prize. Everyone who competes in the games goes into strict training. They do it to get a crown that will not last; but we do it to get a crown that will last forever."

The Devil's goal is to trick us into giving up and he will stop at nothing. But our strength to overcome comes from God and is stronger than any assault Satan can muster. For a man who had spent his entire adult life preaching and teaching the Word, Pastor Jeremiah suddenly seemed out of his element. Ministering to the hearts of lost sheep kept him young, but now, admittedly, he *felt old*. Even though he was strongly convinced that God has a place for us when our lives on earth are over, Pastor Jeremiah worried that he might not make it.

This double-mindedness affected nearly everyone around him, as his children and wife were convinced the pastor's heart was not well. In some ways, knowing *it is always the heart*, they were right; the task was now helping them understand it was his spiritual heart and lack of faith, not his physical heart illness, that needed curing. Like many of my patients and their family members, the pastor came with the expectation of needing only a physical heart healing. Yet in reality, it was his spiritual heart that was in greatest need of healing.

Pastor Jeremiah's physical recovery from the stroke was nothing short of amazing. At the time of his hospital discharge, he looked like himself on the outside, but it was still evident that he lacked the confidence on the inside that he had received complete healing. The pastor's eyes—once filled with unshakable faith—were now slightly fearful and focused on physical circumstances, not on the One who had the power to rescue him. The Devil had convinced him that a rich, full life as he had known it was over. The Apostle Paul compares trials to athletes preparing themselves mentally and physically for competition. Athletes become stronger by having their strength tested. Training is not easy; it is hard work. Pastor Jeremiah, however, didn't see his condition so much as a test of faith, but as an end to life.

I encouraged the pastor and his family to speak God's healing out of their mouths and to avoid even thinking defeatist thoughts of illness. It was time for them to ask God to bind their hearts with encouragement and positive thoughts. When training, the greatest temptation is to give up when things get difficult, which is why all believers should carry the following Scripture in their hearts every day: "I can do everything through him who gives me strength" (Philippians 4:13).

As promised in the previously mentioned 1 Corinthians 9:24, when the heart is focused on the goodness of God, we are able to run in such a way that we may win the prize. Pastor Jeremiah's family was encouraged to speak the truth openly and speak with thankful hearts of God's grace and blessings in their lives.

Despite his lifelong preaching of the good news weekly, when the attack became personal for Pastor Jeremiah, even he began to doubt God's love for him. He had an extraordinary ability to preach to others, but was lost when it came time to apply the Word to his life. At times, I am sure, like many of us, he asked himself, "If God loved me, why would He let me go through this season of physical trials?" Perhaps the answer is centered around the reality that when faced with physical problems, we all need to saturate our thoughts and minds with God's Word to reinforce what we know is true and to guard our hearts. The Devil used the pastor's heart problem as a distraction; in this case it turned out to be more of a nuisance than a life-threatening problem. Pastor Jeremiah was made to focus on his illness and the fear of dying, rather than focus on the true heart-healing process that he knew to be true—and about which he had spent a lifetime preaching.

Pastor Jeremiah felt horribly and blamed his feeling bad on the heart problem; yet prior to his discharge, thorough testing confirmed that his physical heart was not the problem. With his physical heart healing, why was Pastor Jeremiah still feeling so badly? No procedure or new medicine would thwart the Devil's attack. The ultimate healing lies in the truth in God's Word. This reaction was like that of many I care for each day: he simply refused to believe me when I told him his physical heart was not the problem.

In Pastor Jeremiah's mind, he simply could not bring himself to an understanding of how a minister might find himself in need of being ministered to. So I began practicing what I had been preaching to his family. I began speaking the encouraging truth of God's Words to the pastor. Gradually, after several visits to my office, I could see the worry dissipate from his furrowed brow. Soon he exclaimed with a smile reminiscent of my very first meeting with the giant of a man,

"Dr. C, I feel like I just heard me preaching." God was reminding the pastor to live by the encouraging Word he preaches. Spiritual heart healing is not instantaneous, and it would take time to fully mend. It was gratifying to begin to see Pastor Jeremiah's heart softening to spiritual healing.

Six weeks later in the office, during a routine follow-up, the pastor—in his most robust voice ever—made it clear that he got it by looking me in the eye, giving me a firm handshake, and stating, "Doc, you are sounding like me now ... you're getting into my line of work, and I want to thank you!"

After knowing me for many years as a doctor capable of fixing his physical heart, he now saw his physician as someone God was using to *heal his whole heart*. Pastor Jeremiah now fully understood the inseparable binding of the physical and spiritual hearts. The grip the Devil had on the pastor's heart had to be released. Satan had to bow at the foot of Jesus. God says to resist Satan, and he will flee from you. The pastor was now on his way to true heart healing, living the Word, leading by his example, one that he learned by going through this trial. The pastor was counting it joy, as illustrated in James 1:2–4: "Consider it pure joy, my brothers, whenever you face trials of many kinds, because you know that the testing of your faith develops perseverance. Perseverance must finish its work so that you may be mature and complete, not lacking anything." Even with his physical heart problems, he could now be a living witness to God's restorative power.

Pastor Jeremiah was more fully healed now than in all the time that I had known him. He now could truly minister to the hearts of his flock from the position of having been there. I thank God for this experience with Pastor Jeremiah because now I truly understand Romans 8:28: "And we know that in all things God works for the good of those who love him, who have been called according to his purpose."

The pastor, like all of us, had come to a better understanding of the depth and power of his faith when it was put to a life-altering test. Although no one knows God's specific plans for us, we know He wants our hearts; and for us to have the desires of our hearts. He wants to use our lives in a special way. I know God turns bad circumstances in life into good ones and uses us in ways of which we may not be aware. I also know He wants to use us as examples of good health, so that His light can shine through us even in times of difficulty.

Imagine how many lives will now turn to Jesus when they hear the pure conviction in the booming voice of Pastor Jeremiah shining in the summer night, loudly proclaiming the message of Christ's healing power!

Chapter 8

Living in Denial

If we endure, We shall also reign with Him. If we deny
Him, He will also deny us.

—**2 Timothy 2:12 (NKJV)**

Of all the stressful moments common to the work of a cardiologist, the
most difficult is being on call. It is not uncommon to hear the phone ring
in the middle of the night, awakening from a sound sleep to hear the ER
physician tell me the patient is having a heart attack and needs me at
the hospital ASAP. Time is heart muscle, and the faster the heart artery
is opened with a balloon and stent and the heart attack is interrupted,
the better the patient's chance of survival. At the time of the phone call,
it would be hard to consider it a blessing; however, I do consider it a
blessing to have become a part of the lives of many patients via a late-
night call to help them in their coronary emergency. They may have had
no known heart disease and in most cases had no clue what was about
to happen. One minute they were feeling well; the next minute they were
feeling a severe tightness and pressure sensation radiating to the left arm
and neck, making it harder and harder for them to breathe. Drenched
in sweat, many have said they feel as though they are smothering, and
at times feel like they are going to "go out"—a sensation they have
never felt before. Down deep, knowing it must be their heart, their first
instinct is that this can't be so.

Truth is, however, it can be so. We are all often only inches away from the threshold of life to death—all day, every day—and only through God's grace do we avoid crossing the threshold. During a heart attack, as the symptoms gradually worsen, we can almost see the final moment as we find ourselves perilously close to stepping over the line and the fear of dying sets in. It is then that paramedics are called to begin the lifesaving process of rapidly getting people to the emergency room to save them. This is how Jean Watson became one of my patients as I was awakened by the ER doctor at 2:45 a.m.

Jean remembered how the loud yelping siren of the ambulance was drowned out as she focused intently on the irregular beep of her heart on the heart monitor that was hooked up to her chest. She could feel each irregular beat in her throat as she worried each beat would be her last. Jean admitted she was *bargaining with God* during the ambulance ride to keep the beats going. She feared at any moment that she would hear the flat constant hum from the monitor signifying her heart had stopped beating.

Jean recalls talking to God and wishing she had talked to Him before she was in such need. God wants our hearts; and while Jean was a Christian and knew about Christ, she was not really sure if she truly knew Him. She did not turn to Him in her daily life. She had prayed to God, but had she really surrendered her life over to follow Him? Did Jean really know about the storehouse of blessings He wanted to pour out on her life? As long as we have life, it does not matter when we come to Christ, as long as we do, so it is never too late. Even in the critical state in which she found herself, this heart attack had provided Jean with a second chance to change her life. If she survived, Jean now had the chance to turn to Him in worship and prayer. She would learn that a heart truly focused on Christ would be quick to turn to Him in prayer.

Jean had never understood that God loves for us to need Him in every part of our daily lives, not just in times of need like this. No one had ever told her to commit her day to the Lord and pray her way through life's good and bad moments in order to experience the closeness of His presence.

Jean's introduction to a cardiologist like me wasn't unusual; she was very similar to the majority of the people who become patients as a result of an emergency like hers. Many things about a blocked artery will be different, but the need to save a life is always the same. At sixty-one years old, she had smoked heavily for most of her life, and the effects of her habit had started to show up gradually as shortness of breath. In her first statement of denial, Jean attributed her breathing difficulty to getting older and not exercising. She never blamed her cigarettes for affecting her life in any way. When I pressed her, Jean—a rather thin, raspy-voiced, overtly wrinkled woman—admitted to being fatigued and winded with activities that in years past were effortless.

Down deep, Jean knew she needed to stop smoking but could not find the willpower to try. There was a brief period several years earlier when Jean put the cigarettes down. At other times, she claimed she had "cut way back," but because of various stresses in her life, she had started back "because of my nerves," she quickly explained. Although Jean did not realize it (or perhaps did not want to admit it), the Devil was at work in her life, keeping her distracted by his many lies, which resulted in her truly believing she could not overcome this habit. Smoking was only one of many obstacles keeping Jean from enjoying a healthy life. She was too busy to exercise, and her diet consisted of what was convenient.

Usually, convenient food actually means fatty fast food or prepackaged microwavable boxes that temporarily fill the stomach but fall woefully short of providing the body with substantial nutrition. At this point in her life, it was time for Jean to know what God says about us getting control of our lives. She needed to know the truth of God's Word as stated in Proverbs 3:5–6: "Trust in the LORD with all your heart and lean not on your own understanding; in all your ways acknowledge him, and he will make your paths straight." We must be fueled by faith to witness His power at work in our lives—in the same manner that our bodies are fueled from the nutritious food God gives us. This faith-fuel must come from the daily feeding of our hearts with the message of God's Word.

In the case of her life-threatening cigarette habit, Jean's smoking was not the enemy she battled as much as the reasons why she was smoking.

When she arrived in the emergency room, the doctor and nurses worked quickly to get her ready for the cardiac cath lab, where a balloon would soon be inserted to crush the blockage, restore flow to her heart muscle, and in effect, save her life. Jean would soon be on the road to physical heart health healing, yet like so many in this situation, Jean was a long journey away from spiritual heart health. The cath lab was cold, the table was hard, her chest pressure was smothering; but none of that mattered when she experienced the warming relief of a new beginning when the heart attack was interrupted with the balloon. Next, the stent was inserted to complete the repair of the artery at the blockage site, making it difficult to tell there had ever been a problem. Jeremiah 18:1–6 talks about God being the potter and us the clay. God uses life's pressures to mold us, and it was time for Jean to allow God to mold her into the person He wanted her to be.

It is amazing how many times patients will cry out to God to save them in times like these. Then, after receiving a miraculous physical heart healing, many will return home only to fall into the same trap they were in before the heart attack. Some are temporarily motivated, but do not truly commit to God and ultimately succumb to the battle of fighting the Enemy on their own. The Holy Scriptures remind us we are not alone in our battles as confirmed in Exodus 14:14: "The LORD will fight for you; you need only to be still."

God molds and shapes us in different ways. We must allow Him to prune back the deadwood in order that we bloom more fully in the next season. This pruning is difficult and hurts while it is stripping us of bad habits, but it is necessary to achieve true spiritual healing. While hospitalized, insulated from life's troubles, Jean was determined to succeed. After all, she was now three days without a cigarette. "Can you believe it?" she exclaimed. "Three whole days without a cigarette!" The key to her permanently kicking the habit would be for Jean to rely on Him in her daily struggles, instead of her own fragile will. In fact, for the rest of her life, she would always need to turn to Him for sheltering from the constant lies of the Devil.

Upon going home, things were a little easier for Jean, with friends bringing over dinners to help her ease back into her life. Her boss at the local convenience store where she worked gave her two weeks to fully heal from her heart attack. Even the turmoil with her husband, Mack, was better at first. Jean began cardiac rehab and would religiously exercise three times weekly on the monitored treadmills. However, the other four days per week, Jean fell back into her old habits, saying she just didn't feel like exercising. Jean did not realize that doing the right things to receive good health cannot be just a feeling.

We cannot wait to *feel like* exercising or developing good eating habits. It is something that we know is beneficial to our healthy lives, and we must trust that God will be with us and reward us for our faithfulness with heart health healing. Jean had to use this transition period to do the hard work of changing her lifestyle by developing good habits. It was something Jean would not be able to do on her own; she would need God's help to overcome her addictions. Developing the discipline to exercise daily, to eat healthy foods, and to stop smoking would not be optional in order for her to achieve these goals. Soon, the focus and attention Jean received immediately after the heart attack subsided, and she mistakenly felt all alone. Jean had fallen back into the same familiar pattern of living as before her emergency procedure.

Jean looked relatively well—but looks can deceive. She *looked normal*, as if nothing had ever happened to her. The quiet relationship with her husband, Mack, did not last and was once again lost when they both reverted back to their selfish ways of me first. It was evident they both spent a great deal of time focusing on the other's bad qualities, so they chose to coexist but be apart. Jean even blamed Mack for stressing her out so much that she once again resumed smoking her usual one pack per day. Obviously, this was not the manner in which God had intended to mold her.

Upon returning to work, the stresses and overtime hours at the convenience store allowed her to conveniently resurrect her plethora of too-tired-to-exercise excuses.

Jean was exhausted when she got home from work, and what she had learned in cardiac rehab was soon forgotten. Her good intentions went with her each evening when she retired to the recliner. She had no time to learn heart-healthy cooking and felt overwhelmed shopping for the right foods in the grocery store. She simply announced that she had never been good at preparing balanced meals. In essence, she was convinced it was too late for change. "What good would it be for me to change now after all the years of living the way I have?" she asked. This is the Devil's picture-perfect plan: to invite us to a pity party. Not only does he convince us that it is too late to change physically, but how can God ever accept us after all we have said and done?

It had only been two short months since that life-or-death moment in the ambulance when Jean's heart was at its closest point to God at a time when she was dying. At that moment, she was ready to do anything just to live but—despite the best of intentions—she was now as far from Him and spiritual heart health as she ever was. She wanted all God's blessings released in her life—without having to put all the baggage aside.

Now that she was alive, her shaky foundation in God's truth made it difficult for her to find the right path to live forever. At her sixty-day follow-up after hospital discharge, I could smell the lack of progress in the exam room. It is not hard to understand how cigarettes make my patients short of breath. After being enclosed for a half hour or so in a twelve-by-twelve exam room that reeks of tobacco smoke, I, too, find it difficult to breathe! Candidly, I wanted to keep the door open to air out the room and give us both a chance to breathe.

Jean's lack of progress at starting over made it difficult even to tell if her physical heart were okay. It would have been rhetorical if I had asked her how she was doing, as it was clear she was not doing well and had more symptoms now than she did while having the heart attack. God does not want us to primarily focus on our circumstances, but to have faith He is with us and will help us overcome in all situations. All Jean could talk about were the stresses and struggles of her current circumstances. She had made no attempt to become grounded in God. To know Him, we have to get to *know Him*. Developing a relationship with Him takes time and effort, just like staying healthy takes time and effort. The Devil is out to eliminate our personal time with God. God wants to reveal His glory and goodness to us, but it is necessary to spend time with His Word in order to arm ourselves to battle the Devil's lies. God wants to bind us to Himself. When we turn to Him, God wraps Himself around us, intertwining our hearts with His. This is the same binding that occurs when we bind our spiritual and physical hearts. He wants us to look like Him and talk like Him, and when we strive for this—and He puts His hand over our lives—we make it impossible for Satan to attack us. Like many of us, spiritual heart healing was difficult for Jean. She had never thought of God in these terms before. Jean found it hard to understand that God wants an intimate relationship with us and that He talks to our hearts.

With the myriad of symptoms Jean was experiencing, it seemed like an insurmountable task to sort through each of the issues to find the root of her problem. I saw the worry, discouragement, and doubt in her heart reflected in her eyes. As our conversation went back to the night of her heart attack—comparing today's chest pain and shortness of breath—it was clearly different from what she had experienced that night.

Satan has the same method of attack. He is the great deceiver, so helping Jean discern the lies from truth was the primary objective. Knowing her heart and trusting His guidance in my life, I was confident I could help her navigate through the rough waters that were tossing her life in all directions. Above all else, I knew Jean would have to have a determined sense of resolve and a Job-like faith in knowing her redeemer lives. Her walk with God would start with one small reluctant step after another. She would need the support of like-minded and like-faith people around her as she started this journey. Once her roots were firmly established, she could then carefully remove the props and stand firm in the truth presented to us in Hebrews 12:12–13: "Therefore, strengthen your feeble arms and weak knees. 'Make level paths for your feet,' so that the lame may not be disabled, but rather healed." The journey would not be easy, and the Devil would use life's stresses as obstacles that she would need to overcome. Nothing in life is easy; even the farmer knows it is hard work to raise a field for planting, but the harvest is worth it all.

Spending time on the uplifting message of God's love for us, I could see the softening of Jean's heart. At this time, no testing was needed and no procedures were done; but with thirty minutes of focusing more on her spiritual than physical heart, Jean appeared to have begun feeling better. I encouraged her to remember the feeling she had on the night in the ambulance. That night she was bargaining fast and furiously to turn her physical and spiritual life around. It was time to resist the Devil. Going forward, Jean would be running a race that was clearly marked by eating properly, exercise, and no smoking. At the end of the day, she would be able to state with confidence, "I have fought the good fight, I have finished the race, I have kept the faith" (2 Tim. 4:7).

God commands us to be good stewards of all that He gives us. When we give the first fruits of our time to the Lord, He rewards us with all the time and money that we need. Jean's job—no different than any of our jobs—would be to deal with the pressures of life from a position of faith and not fear. We are reminded of this in Philippians 4:7: "And the peace of God, which transcends all understanding, will guard your hearts and your minds in Christ Jesus."

Whether Jean will ultimately be able to conquer the cigarette habit (a conquest that will be particularly joyous for me, since I will no longer have to endure the rigors of the smoky exam room) and maintain a good exercise effort will depend entirely on her ability to keep her eyes fixed upon Jesus. Perhaps the greatest change she will need to undertake will be initiating and maintaining a daily fellowship with God—truly getting to know Him. Psalm 55:22 assures of His watching over us when we give our lives and problems over to Him: "Cast your cares on the LORD and he will sustain you; he will never let the righteous fall." Jean's neglect of her physical heart nearly cost her her life here on earth. Her denial of the need to cultivate a healthy spiritual heart nearly cost her her eternal life. In my opinion, the two simply can not be separated.

Chapter 9

Living in Fear of Dying

Keep your heart with all diligence, For out of it spring the issues of life.

—Proverbs 4:23 (NKJV)

An exhausted, yet anxious, forty-five-year-old Jim walked into the exam room after several sleepless nights and an endless stream of twelve-hour workdays. Like the everyday stresses and strains in his life, his symptoms were not really new. In fact, as I would find out later in the exam, they had been steadily building for quite some time—perhaps even years. Part of my job was to determine what finally pushed him into my office that day and not months earlier.

He did not really know where to start, so he began erratically telling me fragmented bits of information about an overwhelming number of complaints. He nervously answered yes to nearly every question I asked about the symptoms he had been experiencing. I could tell that Jim was living in mortal fear of the answer to the question that actually brought him in to see me. My usual open-ended question "So, what's the real reason you came in today?" was actually the wrong way to start with him, as his fear made it difficult to decipher his symptoms. I knew Jim thought it was his heart even before giving me the chance to sort through his issues. His fear was very understandable, and in his mind very real—especially in light of his family's struggles with the ravages of heart disease. "Big Jim," his one hundred-pounds-plus-overweight, chain-smoking father, died at a young age fifty-three of a massive heart attack and his father's sister just dropped dead at the unthinkably young age of forty-five from what he described as "some sort of heart problem."

So in Jim's mind, it must have been his heart that was making him feel so badly. Interestingly, with the exception of his family history, Jim did not have numerous other cardiac risk factors that made it more likely for him to follow the pathway to early death like his father. Fortunately Jim, unlike his father, had never put a cigarette to his mouth. Despite not eating right or exercising daily, he was not as overweight as you or I might expect. Of course, like countless patients, his years of boxed-sugar breakfasts and fast-food lunches had been staunchly defended and justified by a busy lifestyle. As a testament to his poor diet, recent lab results from his primary care physician revealed a moderately elevated blood sugar, which prompted his doctor to give him a prescription for a "blood-sugar medicine," which, nearly a month later, he had forgotten to fill. A clearly dejected Jim claimed, "I have a cholesterol problem, too," even though he could not recall the specific levels from the recent cholesterol check. It took a considerable amount of time and effort to sort through the myriad of symptoms distressing Jim, yet I was finally able to establish a reasonable understanding of the ailment that prompted this encounter.

As we began talking calmly and rationally about the spiritual side of his symptoms, Jim was not listening. Down deep, he knew his lifestyle was not consistent with God's Word of caring for your body. "Don't you know that you yourselves are God's temple and that God's Spirit lives in you?" (1 Corinthians 3:16). Fear had blinded Jim, and he did not know where to start.

Clearly, Jim was not following God's command to care for his heart. His never-ending days and nights of work had convinced him that his life was permanently stuck in a deep rut, with no way of climbing out. Things of the world had become the centerpiece of his life.

Even though claiming to be a Christian and knowing in his heart he was working for the wrong boss, he made no effort to have a daily relationship with God.

It was little wonder that chest pain, pressure, tightness, shortness of breath, and palpitations seemed to rule Jim's life. His day was filled with chasing after the ever-elusive, unobtainable approval of others, when in reality, his focus should have been centered upon pleasing God. "Whatever you do, work at it with all your heart, as working for the Lord, not for men," (Colossians 3:23) repeated itself over and over in Jim's mind—only he did not know how to apply it to his life. God wants a relationship with us through our hearts, but it requires a committed effort to foster this relationship. A relationship with God is like any relationship … it takes work. Jim's relationships at home, work, school, and play were similarly lacking. Up until his visit with me, Jim had been blaming these stressful, unproductive family, friend, and coworker interactions on those around him; he had not looked in the mirror to see the major role he was playing—or not playing—in these unfulfilled relationships.

Like many of us, Jim relied upon what I refer to as *too-busy logic* to explain away his shortcomings. Basically Jim was simply a poor steward of the time God gave him. Exercise was not important to him. For instance, he easily rationalized being too busy to make time for exercise and staunchly claimed to "walk ten miles per day" at work as a foreman at a factory. According to him, the stress in his life came from everything around him and could never possibly be self-induced—especially when his life was encumbered with a demanding boss, a cold and distant wife, and unappreciative kids.

Although he admitted to being glad to have a job, he did not have enough money at the end of the month to cover his bills. He felt that no matter how hard he worked, he found himself living paycheck-to-paycheck, failing to admit his inflated budget was the real problem.

When he talked about stress, he spoke of it as if it were something so unique to his life and job that no one else could understand what he was going through. It was almost like he needed to fully define the word so I could understand precisely what he was talking about. In some ways, Jim was trying to convince me that he was different from me. This scenario is frequently repeated by many young men and women with similar symptoms—albeit with slightly different story lines—who come into my office every day to find out if it is their heart.

Jim has attributed his shortness of breath when rushing or going up stairs to his twenty-pound weight gain over the last year. His twinges of chest pain were fairly unpredictable—mostly at the end of the day, occasionally when driving home from work, and every once in a while waking him from a sound sleep at night. Although the possibility of heart disease would be investigated thoroughly, my years of experience led me to feel that we would find it was not Jim's physical heart at the root of his symptoms. Until God revealed to me the inseparable binding of the spiritual and physical hearts, management of this type of problem as a cardiologist was at times frustrating. The insight I have gained by studying God's Word has made me better able to understand Jim's problem. As he had neglected the issues of the heart, it came as no surprise that Jim felt as though his life were spiraling out of control. The reality, presence, and purpose of Christ were not there.

It was almost evident in Jim's eyes that he was convinced by the Devil that he was in a hopeless situation that he could not change, which blocked him from understanding God's commands in Proverbs 4:20–23: "My son, pay attention to what I say; listen closely to my words. Do not let them out of your sight, keep them within your heart; for they are life to those who find them and health to a man's whole body. Above all else, guard your heart, for it is the wellspring of life."

Upon further questioning during the exam, Jim revealed his exercise consisted of the walking he did at work and weekend yard work—riding a lawnmower. Not surprisingly, Jim's blood pressure was slightly elevated in the office, as Jim once again relied upon his self-deceptive logic to explain that this always happened in the doctor's office. His rationalization was really nothing more than a feeble attempt to disguise his d-e-n-i-a-l ... which, to some degree, is present in all of us. Despite our saying that we really want to know if we are sick, what we really want is *to know everything is okay*. By ignoring or denying there's a problem (or even a smidgen of room for improvement in our lives), denial allows us to think the problem is not really there. When I think about diagnosing a patient like Jim, I often think of a question my brother has often asked me: "How can you tell if someone has heart disease? Everyone looks so normal." In many ways, Jim was no different from any one of us *normal* people walking down the street. As he looked around the waiting room, mostly filled with older patients, he wondered why he was even here—which immediately made him feel better. In another moment of denial, he actually rose from his seat to leave, but was forced to change his mind and stay when he felt an additional twinge of chest pain.

Sorting through Jim's symptoms, there was nothing that had changed recently to prompt his office visit. He had been feeling this way for a very long time, and—weighed down with "Big Jim's" premature death—Jim finally overcame his fears and mustered the courage to ask me the one question to which no one wants to hear an affirmative answer: "Doctor, is it my heart?" Knowing how important the heart is to our lives, coupled with the fact that heart disease is the number one killer of men and women in the United States, makes me marvel at how little attention we give to keeping our hearts in optimal condition. Our lack of attention to a good healthy diet and daily exercise subconsciously eats away at us and burdens or hearts—which finally drives us in to see the doctor.

I directed the conversation to a few Scriptures regarding God's commandment about guarding and taking care of our hearts. Next I took him through the "commandments" of a healthy diet, daily exercise, and the countless other disciplines we should all adhere to for strong healthy hearts. Then, I directed the conversation to the number of times God referenced our hearts in the Bible. I explained in my best non-preachy manner that God would not likely have focused on the heart more than seven hundred times in Scripture if it were not of primary importance to Him. As I shared with him my points about God wanting us to live a life of optimal heart health, I could see by his reactions he had never understood it in this way before.

I emphasized that God had revealed to me what I consider to be an undeniable link between our physical and spiritual hearts. I also discussed the fact that the heart is the most important and the hardest-working organ in the body, beating over 100,000 times per day.

Jim's eyes opened slightly wider, his body shifted itself in the chair toward me, and he began to focus on what I was saying. Although he was following me, I could tell he still did not get it. Even though he did not admit his belief in what I was trying to share with him, I interpreted his look as a hopeful moment—in fact, a breakthrough moment that I hoped showed Jim was beginning to finally understand what I felt God wanted me to share with him. However, I realize my job is only to plant the seed. Only time would tell if the seeds had landed in a soft, receptive heart and begun to flourish.

Investing in the development of a strong physical heart requires a commitment to invest ourselves in developing a strong spiritual heart. Why? Because God longs to have a fully developed relationship with us through our hearts—not just a Sunday-morning relationship. In Jim's case, not only was he not investing time in improving his physical heart health; he claimed to not have the time to develop his spiritual heart health. In truth, Jim was simply denying himself the beauty and fullness of a relationship with our Lord. Of course, he always fell back on his plethora of excuses, yet he had no honest reasons as to why it was okay for him to ignore God. As I concluded the exam-room visit, I was hoping that a seed of faith had been planted and that a new outlook on physical and spiritual heart health would provide Jim with the armament to appropriately respond to the physical, mental, and spiritual attacks he was experiencing. In 1 Corinthians 3:6, Paul states, "I planted the seed, Apollos watered it, but God made it grow."

I knew it would be important to help provide Jim with peace of mind via appropriate testing to thoroughly evaluate his physical heart. As I began reviewing the necessary tests to accomplish our goal, Jim's denial resurfaced.

He protested that huge problems would be created down at the plant by his taking off the necessary time for completion of the tests. "My boss is not going to like this at all," he stated very matter-of-factly.

"You're probably right," I quickly responded. "You need to pick the least disruptive day for your boss—and I'm sure you can find the best time."

Jim said nothing, but nodded reluctantly.

Jim came through the tests much better than he expected. Yet, rather than being pleased with the good news of his normal tests, he lapsed back into a nervous, depressed state similar to our first meeting. Shaking his head in disbelief, he muttered, "These symptoms are not my imagination. What the heck is causing my problems?"

Even if there were a simple answer, I knew Jim likely would deny it, much like nearly every other issue in his life. So I began the long, arduous task of focusing on the next part of my relationship with him as his cardiologist: to make him a better steward of the body God had given him. It was time for Jim to begin changing his lifestyle to make it more likely to lead to a long life, which he could live with all God desired for him.

Jim, like so many of us, wanted to enjoy the harvest, but was unwilling to do the hard work of sowing the seeds of change and doing the necessary *plowing of the field* to achieve this bounty. Unfortunately, unless we know what God says about our hearts, commit to learning this truth, and then put it into our daily lives, we will not truly have peace. I am convinced God wants our hearts.

At one time in my life, I did not understand the depth of God's love for me. Until I developed a closer relationship with God through His Word, I did not know how intimately involved He was in my life. I encounter many patients, and even friends, who often deny the fact that God desires close involvement in the health of our bodies and minds. Yet their denial often stands, not only as a barrier between good and bad health, but as an obstacle to enjoying the fullness of His love in our daily lives—and possibly block us from life for eternity.

This relationship starts with us. It takes effort on our parts for our healing and good health. God tells us to come near to Him, so that He will come near to us. "Come near to God and he will come near to you. Wash your hands, you sinners, and purify your hearts, you double-minded" (James 4:8). Although Jim finds himself concerned about heart disease and living a long life, we also find him still unwilling to put forth the efforts to receive the rich blessing of good physical and spiritual heart health. His unwillingness to lay aside the denial lays heavy on his heart and makes itself manifest in the symptoms that Jim is experiencing—chest pain, pressure, heaviness, tightness, palpitations, and shortness of breath. Instead of his starting each day by worrying about the issues consuming his life, it is time for Jim to start his day studying God's Word and saturate his heart with the truth of His love for us. This will take a commitment of time, effort, and concentration to stay focused on Him. Knowing what God says and how He cares for us will motivate us to put forth the effort to exercise daily and commit to healthy meal choices. We must plan our days around time to exercise and time to choose healthier diets. With a full work schedule, time for exercising will need to be made either before or after work.

I personally choose the afterwork schedule to help with stress relief as I fellowship with God during my exercise time. One cannot wait to feel like exercising, or it will not happen. From the nourishment standpoint, it is interesting to note that we feed our bodies three times per day, but nourish our hearts only once per week at best. The same is true about developing our relationships with God. If we find ourselves spending time in His Word only occasionally, how will we know the depth of what God really says about our hearts and lives? It is vital to take nourishment from the pages to feed our heads in order for it to be nourishing to our hearts.

If we do not, we are open to the life-threatening lies of the Devil. In my twenty-five-plus years of experience, an overwhelming majority of my patients agree that this is a true message, and many know the lifelong value of spending time in the Word. Just as exercising and eating right are necessary for a long, healthy life, exercising the heart with a generous measure of God's Word is equally vital. But for many, the obstacle is applying this truth to their lives.

It is an amazing observation that when people have free time on vacation, I see them exercising, apparently for the first time, which shows me down deep in their hearts, they know exercise is beneficial for their health and is rejuvenating to their hearts and minds. It was time for Jim to change his heart, by changing his lifestyle, which would only occur by him losing the denial and finding the real truth to a long life. There is no condemnation in Christ, so Jim must begin slowly, with a plan that works for his life. Jim cannot worry about his progress in comparison to his friends or family, but must stay focused on the plan God has for him.

Jim will hopefully find both comfort and resolve in Hebrews 12:11: "No discipline seems pleasant at the time, but painful. Later on, however, it produces a harvest of righteousness and peace for those who have been trained by it." Jim is where God has him, and it is my job now to encourage him to stay on the path God has marked for him. It may sound like a cliché, but this path, like our life path, is a marathon, and what is important is not how we start out, but how we finish.

Chapter 10

When Is It Over?

It is better to go to a house of mourning than to go to a house of feasting, for death is the destiny of every man; the living should take this to heart.

—Ecclesiastes 7:2

When is it over? This is the question we all will face in our lives—some sooner than others. The answer is something only God knows. He gives us a book full of instruction—much of which encourages us to live our lives as if today is the last day. Matthew 6:34 illustrates the fact that no one is guaranteed tomorrow: "Therefore do not worry about tomorrow, for tomorrow will worry about itself. Each day has enough trouble of its own." We do not know when we will leave this earthly life as we know it. The road does not simply dead-end after our physical death. The Bible makes it perfectly clear in Hebrews 9:27 that we all come to the fork in the road of heaven or hell: "Just as man is destined to die once, and after that to face judgment."

For life everlasting in heaven, God is clear that we cannot make it through works. Things we have done and accumulated during our lives on earth cannot qualify us for admission to heaven; no one is qualified. Rather, it is through His grace and love for us that God gave us His only Son as penance for our sins. By accepting Jesus into our hearts, we receive the gift of life everlasting, of which none of us is worthy. "For God so loved the world that he gave his one and only

Son, that whoever believes in him shall not perish but have eternal life" (John 3:16).

No one on earth is immune to disease. No amount of money or power can buy us out of disease. Eventually, our physical heart dies, and our lives on earth are over. That is why it is literally a matter of eternal life and death to get our spiritual hearts intertwined with God. We must have a soft, receptive heart to God's Word to enjoy all that He has for us here on earth and to be ready for that time when we will face the judgment seat of Christ. We must live as is stated in Psalm119:112: "My heart is set on keeping your decrees to the very end."

Romans 8:36 reminds us that "...we face death all day long; we are considered as sheep to be slaughtered." This Scripture is especially true when it comes to the gravity of heart disease, the number-one killer of men and women in the United States. Just as a healthy spiritual heart is a key to life everlasting, a healthy physical heart—the most important organ in our bodies—is the key to longer life here on earth. The statistics associated with heart disease are staggering. During every minute of every day, one person crosses over from life to death from a heart attack—over 600,000 annually. As a cardiologist, one of the most difficult things to know is whether or not the heart attack the patient is experiencing will be the one from which he or she will not recover. As doctors, we are limited to diagnosing a patient's condition and attempting a prognosis based solely upon that which we can see and hear. The knowledge of the precise moment a patient's physical heart will beat its final beat is a final moment known only by our God. To even try to know that which God knows would undoubtedly be a life-crushing burden for the frail human mind and spirit.

This was the situation facing Mrs. Whitt—Nana as she was known to her family—as she began to have severe substernal chest pain shortly before ten o'clock at night while she was getting ready for bed at the assisted living center where she lived.

She never thought it could be her heart. At eighty-two years old, Mrs. Whitt had mild dementia, which primarily affected her short-term memory, making it hard to live independently—although she still knew and interacted with her caring family well. That night Nana called her granddaughter Nicole in a panic as a smothering chest pain was causing her whole body to struggle to fill her lungs with air. With her long-term memory intact, she remembered thinking that these symptoms were *a thousand times worse* than the heart attack she survived in 1996, which ultimately led to her open-heart bypass surgery. Hunched over from osteoporosis but still quite spry for her age, she had modest limitations in her activities because of arthritis (mostly bothering her knees, hips, and hands). Additionally, her poor eyesight and a slight unsteadiness when walking required her to occasionally use a cane for balance. However, she claimed to "just swing it," not wanting to admit her dependence on a crutch. A widow since her husband died six years previously from a heart attack, Nana's daughters and grandchildren felt assisted living could help give her the independence she desired, while providing help with meals and medicines that she now required because of forgetfulness and activity limitations. Mrs. Whitt considered herself *at home* with her many senior sisters and brothers to remind her she was not alone in her late-in-life struggles. Mrs. Whitt also looked forward to the daily organized activities and mobility improvement exercise class provided by the local senior citizen support group.

Despite her aches, pains, and difficulties, no one was ready for Nana to go—certainly not Nana. In spite of her age, Mrs. Whitt had not spent much time thinking about the end of her life. Granddaughter Nicole immediately called 911, who sent paramedics to *Nana's home* to save her dying grandmother.

Nicole and her mother, Linda, were at the emergency room when the ambulance arrived with Nana, gasping as if for her last breath. Her blood pressure was dangerously low; her skin was cool and clammy, and she was sweating excessively, as if her whole body were struggling to fill her lungs with air. Her heart was beating as hard and as fast as it could as it struggled to pump blood—in shock from the sudden loss of blood flow from a major artery. The ECG confirmed a sudden, severe life-threatening myocardial infarction to the back wall of her heart, which was now forcing Mrs. Whitt and her family to face the question *"Is it over for Nana?"* One minute, Mrs. Whitt was fine; the next, she was facing death from a ruptured plaque and blood clot likely trying to close one of her bypass grafts that had helped keep her alive for the last fourteen years.

Linda and Nicole were tearful as they watched someone dear to them struggle with life—or more realistically, to fight off death. As Mrs. Whitt had grown older, her family had seen her gradual physical and mental decline, especially accelerated over the past year. Her daughter Linda quietly worried and wondered when it would be over for her mama. This question will come to all of us, dealing with our loved ones, and at some point, ourselves. As a cardiologist, I have seen this indescribable moment of fear grip families more times than I can recall ... usually, like with Mrs. Whitt, quite suddenly without warning. It is especially during tense, emotionally charged moments like these that I am thankful God has sent the Counselor to help guide me to the right decisions in caring for His children. With younger patients, we aggressively use all tools and resources available to battle cardiac death. The decision with older patients, however, can be heart-wrenching.

Ecclesiastes 7:2 tells us, "...death is the destiny of every man; the living should take this to heart." I've heard it said that everyone has a date with death.

I believe this unalterable fact of God's universe is why He commands us to keep our minds and hearts focused on His Word, have a personal relationship with Jesus trusting in Him in all things, and delight ourselves in the Lord daily. He does not command us to do these things weekly, monthly, or semiannually—or even every once in awhile; *He says daily.* The reason is very simple to understand. We must be ready for eternity—ready to be welcomed into His kingdom, because at the time of our last heartbeat on earth, it is too late. God's reassuring Word in John 5:24 removes the finality of physical death from life on earth: "'I tell you the truth, whoever hears my word and believes him who sent me has eternal life and will not be condemned; he has crossed over from death to life.'"

Despite her dementia, Nana *knew Jesus,* and she and the family knew where she was going when her life on earth was over. But they could not let go now that her time was near. How did they know this was the end? They could see the life-ending struggle on her face and in her eyes. Were they doing the right thing asking the doctors and nurses to try to save her life with an emergency balloon and stent? If she stopped breathing, should they allow a tube to be inserted into her airway to help her breathe? After all, the family repeated, "Mama didn't want to be kept alive on a ventilator."

Mrs. Whitt was in cardiac shock, with her heart—and body—failing moment by moment from this heart attack. There was a 100 percent chance of physical death without opening the artery with a stent. I shared the fifty-fifty survival odds with the family even if we were successful with the stent, while concurrently telling them that death was imminent if we didn't proceed right away. This life-and-death decision was too overwhelming for Linda and Nicole to make. As Mrs. Whitt's heart doctor, it was necessary to use godly judgment to help guide the family through the burdensome task of what to do.

Mrs. Whitt's overall quality of life was reasonably good, and she was happy in spite of her physical and mental limitations. Knowing Mrs. Whitt trusted in the Lord as her Savior comforted everyone that her life after death would be assured. She did not need any time to get her spiritual heart right. Since she enjoyed a reasonably good overall quality of life, there was an overwhelming peace at proceeding with emergency arteriogram and balloon and stent to open up the offending artery in an attempt to save her physical life. Experience has shown me the regret and remorse a family faces if they have even an ounce of doubt that they did everything they could to save the life of a loved one. I have seen times where there was no procedure, no medicine, no amount of money, nor any other means of rescue to save the life of the patient when his or her predestined time on earth had come to an end. There are also times when it is equally evident that nothing could or should be done to save a life—but Nana's case was clearly not one of those times.

Three years prior to the emergency she currently faced, Mrs. Whitt had unstable angina—not a heart attack—that caused severe chest pain. However, it was not nearly as much pain as she was experiencing now. At that time, the bottom artery bypass graft had a 95 percent blockage that was successfully stented. The front artery bypass was closed at some unknown earlier time and was managed with medications, while the bypass graft to the back artery—the one that was now causing problems—was open, without significant blockages. At that point, a three-years-younger Mrs. Whitt had better overall blood flow to her heart, which allowed us to fix her problem and have her back on her feet the next day. The arteriogram this time was much different. The previously stented bypass from 2007 had now closed without Mrs. Whitt knowing it. Linda stated, "Nana never complained of chest pain or shortness of breath."

This can happen gradually over time without symptoms and is not an unusual occurrence. It is not uncommon for the heart to tolerate changes that happen slowly, and it compensates to reroute the blood flow and Mrs. Whitt never knew this had happened. The sudden change now was a 99 percent blockage with sluggish blood flow in her last remaining bypass graft to the back artery. For any chance at continuing her physical life, a balloon-stent to open and repair the bypass graft was vitally important. The procedure was accomplished successfully; but in my heart—given her age, medical issues, and now arteriogram results—I knew Nana was perilously close to the edge of life on earth. Even if she survived this heart attack, with Nana's physical heart, coupled with her current health condition and age, I was certain she would not be able to go through this again.

In my heart, I knew that this was the last procedure Mrs. Whitt would have. It would be comforting to the family and the doctor to know we did all that we could do. A comforting Scripture, Isaiah 57:1–2, came to mind as I stood in the center of her hospital room surrounded by her family: "The righteous perish, and no one ponders it in his heart; devout men are taken away, and no one understands that the righteous are taken away to be spared from evil. Those who walk uprightly enter into peace; they find rest as they lie in death." Everyone was at peace with pursuing the path to try to save Nana's life.

There was peace with Mrs. Whitt and her family, no matter the result of this heart attack. They just wanted to know they followed God's plan for her life. They knew she would *live* either way. Peace comes from within. Mrs. Whitt and her family had peace even during the most traumatic and uncertain times during her heart attack. This is the type of peace when—in spite of our sins—we know the peace of Jesus is in our hearts.

It's the peace that Jesus made with God for us outlined in Isaiah 53:12: "Therefore I will give him a portion among the great, and he will divide the spoils with the strong, because he poured out his life unto death, and was numbered with the transgressors. For he bore the sin of many, and made intercession for the transgressors." God is always our comforter. There is never a time even during death when we are alone.

By immediately restoring blood flow to the back wall of Mrs. Whitt's heart, there were signs of physical improvement, but she was still critically ill. Time is always God's harvest in our lives, and time would show whether opening the bypass graft would give Nana more time on earth. With time, God's plan always becomes quite clear. By early the next morning, more medicines were needed to maintain her blood pressure. The cardiac shock she had experienced only twenty-four hours before was now resulting in multiple organ failure, and it was obvious nothing and no one could stop the inevitable.

In retrospect, even successfully stenting this bypass vessel did not save her life. There is no fighting God's plan. There is no disease, diagnosis, or difficulty God can't handle, but at some point in everyone's life, there is an appointed time for our dates with physical death. In light of this, our only focus should be to trust in His assurances of life everlasting. His light shines through us in all circumstances. The family gathered, prayed, and walked away from her bedside with the peace that they had followed God's plan for Nana's life. Despite the loss of her physical presence, they trusted God's Word that they would see her again in heaven—equally assured that she would no longer be suffering. "We are confident, yes, well pleased rather to be absent from the body and to be present with the Lord" (2 Corinthians 5:8 NKJV).

"When is it over?" is a question to which no one has the answer.

We are truly blessed in each minute of life on earth and are justified by faith in our Lord Jesus Christ. God's Word has the final say in life. To make sure we spend eternity with God, we must spend time knowing and living His Word here on earth. "For the word of God is living and active. Sharper than any double-edged sword, it penetrates even to dividing soul and spirit, joints and marrow; it judges the thoughts and attitudes of the heart. Nothing in all creation is hidden from God's sight. Everything is uncovered and laid bare before the eyes of him to whom we must give account" (Hebrews 4:12–13).

Ideally, we would love to live a long, healthy, fruitful physical life well into our eighties and nineties. By actively pursuing Him, taking care of our physical bodies, and keeping our focus on His Word, we receive all the blessings He has for us on earth and ensure ourselves a place of life ever after with God in heaven. To get there, we must put our trust and faith in Jesus, and we must have God's Word to know Jesus in our lives.

He instructs us to come boldly to the throne with the grace of Christ to find mercy. "For it is by grace you have been saved, through faith— and this not from yourselves, it is the gift of God—not by works, so that no one can boast" (Ephesians 2:8–9). Grace is the power that comes only from humbling ourselves before Christ. That is why the proud simply do not get it. Trying to do it on our own is acting in pride. We must repent to get in His will for our lives.

The question *"When is it over?"* is a universal question pondered by every man and woman from every culture on the face of the planet as they grow older. Personally, I think of it as a distraction.

We all know the Devil likes to distract us from the will of God, worrying about how much time we have left, rather than thankfully living each blessed day as a gracious witness of the glory of God.

I have been encouraged to think about life, to know His Word, and to accept Jesus as Lord, so not only do I enjoy each day of life on earth, but I am assured of life in heaven when my physical life on earth is over. "Jesus said to her, 'I am the resurrection and the life. He who believes in Me, though he may die, he shall live. And whoever lives and believes in Me shall never die...'" (John 11:25–26 NKJV). So, I avoid asking the question. We have no way of knowing the answer, and it only serves to distract us from God's peace. Keeping a focus on Jesus, we will not need to know *when*; more importantly, we will know *where* we are headed when our last heartbeats on earth have come and our physical bodies die. When the physical heart's work is complete, we need to know our spiritual hearts live forever in heaven in the wonderful presence of our Lord and Savior, Jesus Christ.

It's Always the Heart
Is Always About Change

> You were taught, with regard to your former way of life, to
> put off your old self, which is being corrupted by its deceit-
> ful desires; to be made new in the attitude of your minds
>
> **—Ephesians 4:22–23**

By now, we should understand that the physical and spiritual hearts are
intimately intertwined. Truly, one cannot change the physical heart's
attitude and behavior without changing the spiritual heart. We can
control our behaviors for a little while, but unless we change inwardly,
we cannot succeed long-term.

When we know we need to change—whether it is to stop smoking,
change our eating habits, or begin and maintain a daily exercise
program—we have to ask God to change us. Any life change must
begin by turning to God, who knows us beyond our knowledge of
ourselves. Psalm 139:13 is a wonderful passage that details how God
knows everything about us: "For you created my inmost being; you knit
me together in my mother's womb." Why would one not turn to the
potter who made us in His image to mold and change us?

Now we must do our part. We must study in the area of our needs
and pray as we prepare to change our lifestyles. Fellowship with God
all day, so when we hear the lies that encourage us to smoke, overeat,

and not exercise, we immediately thank Him for working behind the scene to change our behaviors. This is something I know I cannot do long-term by myself. Instead of, "I don't feel like exercising," we should say, "Thank You for giving me desire and strength and a healthy body so I can exercise."

Look around you; many people with much less are doing more than you! The problem is we have to change the way we think. James 4:2 tells us, "…You do not have, because you do not ask God."

Do you ask God for help and thank Him for working in your life when you need help, or do you try to do things in your own strength? I do not try to change myself, because it will not be a lasting change.

We have to learn to ask God, who lives in our hearts. John 15:7 says, "If you remain in me and my words remain in you, ask whatever you wish, and it will be given you." We are to make Him, not the things we are trying to change, the focus of our lives. He wants us to "…bear fruit—fruit that will last. Then the Father will give you whatever you ask in my name" (John15:16). There is *authority* in the name of Jesus. We do not go in our own strength. Presenting in the name of Jesus for His glory opens the door for God to do great things in our lives. Even though we do not deserve it, ask for the outrageous promises from God. When I come in Jesus' name, John 14:13 (NKJV) promises, "And whatever you ask in My name, that I will do, that the Father may be glorified in the Son."

Apart from Him, we can do nothing. So why not turn our burdens over to Him? God is the God of hearts. He wants us to talk with Him daily, asking all day long, as illustrated in John 16:23–24: "…my Father will give you whatever you ask in my name … Ask and you will receive, and your joy will be complete." Be willing to put yourself in the hands of the potter.

He makes us what He wants us to be. Once we get our hearts right and know we depend on God for guidance in all matters in our lives, it will be easier to begin and maintain a lifestyle that gives us the best chance for success, no matter the physical limitations.

The benefits of exercise to one's life and health are well documented. Daily exercise not only improves heart health, but is beneficial *treatment* for many other diseases, including the mobility-limiting conditions of osteoporosis and arthritis. The first question is how to get started. The main thing is to make it a priority to take better care of ourselves. This takes planning. Some people find it best to start the day off exercising, while others find it best to go in the late afternoon or early evening after work, while yet others have a schedule that allows them to choose the time each day that best suits their hearts. For me, my mind and body are best suited to commit to exercising in the evening during weekdays after leaving work. The perils associated with end-of-day exercise become family or work commitments that sap the time and energy set aside for exercise. With planning, this derailing can be kept to a minimum.

On weekends and when on vacation, my days are more flexible, and I can make the decision about when to exercise around my free time. For my wife, Mary, whose schedule is more flexible, she can select different times to exercise best suited for her varied schedule; however, she rarely if ever compromises this commitment and spends an hour or more each day exercising. I encourage each of us to honestly assess and choose the time that gives the best chance to succeed.

Mary Tallent at eighty years old goes to bed after the nightly news, rises at 6:00 a.m. each day, has her quiet time with God, and prefers to walk her three miles in forty-five-plus minutes at seven thirty each morning—rain or shine. She prefers to walk on the track at the local college in her small town, sometimes walking with friends. She enjoys going to the college to walk as it brightens her day to be around other people she encounters while exercising.

Mr. Important, with his tendency to get tied up with important business issues as the day progresses, should consider an early-morning exercise routine. This would give him time to think about the upcoming events of his day and to focus on the things he needs to do to help him organize his day. Alternatively, he might find the stress relief of evening exercise helps him unwind, review the events of the day, and plan for the next day. This would allow his early-morning time to be devoted to fellowshipping with the Lord, humbling him and readying him for the stresses to come.

Like Mary Tallent, Jim Oliver—Mr. Commitment, who is very committed to changing his life—prefers early morning fellowship with God and then exercise in the morning at his local YMCA. This allows him to mix cardio and light weight training, where he commits at least forty-five minutes daily to his regimen—which has become much easier now that he is mostly retired.

For those who work outside the home, like Fearful-Heart Jim, Searching Joanne, Jacob the electrician, Jean the convenience store cashier, and Pastor Jeremiah, the timing of daily exercise will be a function of determining how early they need to get up in the morning for work relative to how late they get home.

These determinants are essential in choosing the best time to commit to daily exercise.

Although the job of a long-haul truck driver like Leroy Harris presents its own set of unusual circumstances, he too will have to modify his schedule to make time for daily exercise. Whether he rises earlier in the morning to faithfully walk around the motel parking lot or pulls his rig off the highway thirty minutes earlier than before, his better health and clear mind will more than make up for the loss of road time.

For those like Mrs. Whitt, in the very late stages of life, muscle-strengthening and mobility exercises are particularly important to help them get around; these exercises will give them a sense of accomplishment and improve their mental focus. The emaciated Jacob the deceiver just needs to walk daily to clear his head and talk to God. This committed regimen will serve to instill much-needed discipline into his life.

This brings us to the type of exercise I am professing as beneficial to our minds and bodies. This will be different for everyone dependent upon the age, limitations in mobility, and state of conditioning— yet the basic principle of committing to thirty to forty-five minutes of some sort of brisk aerobic activity is always the same. Realistically, counting warm-up, cool-down, and so on, one must set aside one to one and one-half hours for this process. The form of exercise can range from brisk walking, biking, swimming, spin classes, jogging or running, rowing, biking or stationary biking, water aerobics, or stairstepping to many low-impact gliders, which are easier on the joints. I personally enjoy jogging; however, I am also incorporating muscle and core-strengthening, low-impact aerobics, light weights, sit-ups and push-ups, and cardio classes into my weekly routine. As we get older, strengthening our muscles helps us overcome the effects of the natural loss of muscle mass as we age.

Strengthening our muscles will help us throughout the day with routine activities such as going up stairs, carrying groceries, and even getting out of a chair; moreover, it will also make our exercise routines easier and more enjoyable to complete.

If people have not exercised and are just getting started, I recommend they get a clearance from their physicians. They must begin slowly, ultimately increasing the pace that makes it challenging to carry on a conversation while exercising. Some people have the needs and resources available to get one-on-one personal instruction to develop a plan best suited for them. This can come in the form of personal certified trainers or through classes at the local gym or YMCA memberships.

Obviously this subject is multifaceted and deserves much more discussion, as well as adjustments made as experiences broaden. I encourage you to learn more at the *It Is Always the Heart* website and instructional manuals.

A good nutritious low-fat low-cholesterol diet is also a subject worthy of a book in and of itself. Again, it takes a change of heart to succeed at learning what foods are good for our hearts and bodies and devising nutritious ways of preparation to suit each individual taste. We have to learn to love healthy eating. There are several *uncompromising principles.*

One of the most important rules to adhere to is to always avoid fast food. Fast food is usually unhealthy, prepared in an unhealthy way, and is usually not as satisfying as a healthy serving of a lean meat and three (vegetables). Turning to fast-food meals results from poor planning and time management. All are given the same twenty-four hours in a day by God, and it is our responsibility to be good stewards of that time.

There has to be a commitment to preparation. One has to prepare to eat right. For some, this may require cooking meals for the entire week, refrigerating or freezing and using as the need arises. For me, I like to use leftovers from a previous night's meal, put them in Tupperware, and bring them to work the next day. Another important rule is to avoid anything boxed, bagged, or microwaved for the same reasons as you should avoid fast foods. Also detrimental to a healthy body and heart is the habit of eating snacks late at night before going to bed, when metabolism is at its lowest.

A sub-rule to this one, the size of our meals should be biggest at breakfast, less at lunch, and least at dinner—just like an inverted triangle—or our bodies will take *the shape of a triangle*, with our bellies and backsides as the base of the triangle. Consuming enough water throughout the day is a necessity to stay well-hydrated and assist in digestion. As a general rule, every day one should drink one half of an ounce of water for each pound of ideal body weight (90 oz for a 180-lb person).

Many people I see look to what I will refer to as fad diets—those diet plans to help people lose weight more quickly—yet these schemes are rarely successful long-term. The weight loss will not last, as these diets are not sustainable for healthy living long-term. They are a shortcut for instant gratification that takes time and effort, yet spending the same time and effort to learn how to best fuel our bodies with the nutritious foods God gave us will provide lasting results to help us prosper.

Balance is the key: stick with fruits, vegetables, lean meats, fish, nuts, and grains, which will help us look healthier and be better nourished.

It is difficult to count calories in a day; however, having a general idea of the calories needed in a day to maintain a certain ideal body weight, keeping the fat content of our diets less than 30 percent of the total number of calories, knowing unsaturated fats are better for us than saturated fats, keeping the total cholesterol less than 300 milligrams per day, drinking plenty of water, and avoiding processed foods will provide a groundwork for a healthy mind, body, and heart, which can be used to bring God glory.

We spend so much time avoiding what we know we should do for healthy living. If we would only do what we are supposed to do, when we are supposed to do it—and get done that which we are supposed to get done—God will show us what needs to be done in our lives. Christianity is all about developing and nurturing a personal ongoing relationship with Christ. All of us are guilty of letting other things crowd our faith.

All of us are very good at making excuses as to why we cannot follow God's truth—too busy, preoccupied, booked up, overcommitted, important, comfortable, scared, or simply spread too thin. His Word teaches us everything we need to know about life. It is time to open our eyes and hearts so we can see what our loving God wants us to understand—*it is always the heart!*

It's Always The Heart

Diet Recommendations For a Healthy Heart

The diet/weight loss industry is a big business in this country that has conditioned the public to believe that their "plan" is the only successful plan for losing weight. So, when my patients ask for recommendations for a heart-healthy diet, it is understandable that they expect me to present them with a type of "plan" that requires – among other things– complicated calculations of points, calories, volume, etc. of nearly every morsel of food they eat. Instead, I offer them a heart-healthy diet that is not at all complicated.

Also, they quickly learn I am an advocate of "real" vs. "fake". Noticeably absent from my suggested diet are microwave meals and processed foods. Margarine doesn't have a place in my refrigerator – only real butter. With the exception of rice or pasta – I don't recommend anything from a box (I know the "helper" meals might be quick and tasty…but there are better choices that are much better for you). God blessed us with an abundance of healthy, natural foods – many of which are as "quick to eat" as the sodium and sugar-heavy foods with tons of additives that have contributed to America's growing obesity-related health problems.

So with a generous helping of common sense, and perhaps a slight nod to my Greek heritage, I present the following sample 7-day diet as a starting point for our journey to a healthy physical and spiritual heart.

Breakfast	Lunch	Dinner
2 Scrambled Eggs (with peppers, onions, feta cheese-or other cheese), 1 slice wheat toast, 1fruit, 8 oz. milk	3-5 oz. Tuna fish salad on whole wheat bread, small salad or grilled chicken on bed of salad + fruit	4-6 oz. Grilled (cook on grill) chicken + salad and potato wedges baked w/ seasoning/ herbs
6 oz. Greek yogurt +/-honey with fruit (straw, blue, black berries, pineapple), nuts, pumpkin/bran muffin.	Sat/Sun leftover with salad, water	6-8 oz. Baked or pan-fried in olive oil salmon, one cup fresh spinach cooked in olive oil, sweet potatoes-baked whole or sliced pan-fried in olive oil/ herb seasoning, whole wheat roll w/olive oil + herbs
Fried eggs 2 with onion, avocado (butter or olive oil), wheat toast, milk.	3-4 oz. thinly sliced turkey sandwich, 1 cup vegetable soup, nuts	3-5 oz. Chicken and rice, 1 cup spinach salad, 1 cup sautéed carrots and onions in wine, butter or olive oil)
6 oz. Yogurt +/- wheat germ, banana, 1 slice wheat toast with avocado, nuts , OJ	Monday leftovers with salad	3-6 oz. baked Ziti, small salad, 1 thin-slice bread with olive oil and spice seasonings.
2 hard boiled eggs, turkey bacon, milk + muffin (pumpkin / bran)	Tues leftovers with salad	2-3 Fajitas (chicken) with black-beans, corn –pan-fried w butter or olive oil.
6 oz. of Greek yogurt w/ 1 piece of fruit, 1 slice wheat toast w/ avocado	Wed leftovers with salad	6-8 oz of another fish- cod, orange roughly, grouper breaded and pan-fried with salad, 1 cup squash + onions
1 cup Whole grain cereal with 8 oz. milk (or oatmeal w/ honey), with nuts and fruit, 1 slice toasted wheat bread with peanut butter and honey	3-5 oz. Stir fry sesame chicken with 1 cup vegetables or make your own pizza or grilled cheese with salad/stir fry veggies	3-5 oz. Grilled (cook on grill) steak or lean hamburger + small salad and baked potato

Here are a few additional tips to make the most of a healthier approach to your daily diet:

Snacks – don't allow them to be your diet downfall. A small handful of dry-roasted nuts are far better for you than a handful of cookies or salty chips. Popcorn, raw veggies, fruit, and even a small baked-potato are a great source of between meal energy and make for a healthy mid-morning or mid-afternoon snack.

Leftovers – they are much faster than fast food. Taking leftovers for lunch saves time and money and represents healthy calories as opposed to the local burger and fries fare. To liven up your leftovers from a previous dinner – prepare a nice salad and add the chicken, steak, fish, burger or tuna with feta cheese and dressing (you can make your own with oil/vinegar/spices and honey mustard).

Breakfast – it is not an option. Always start your day with breakfast – even if you take it with you on the way to work. Also, take along water, fruit and nuts for snacking.

H20 – I cannot emphasize the importance of water-intake enough – especially over tea, soft drinks, coffee, etc. One ounce of water for half your body weight is a good measurement tool. (Example: 150 lbs. total body weight ÷ 2 = 75 oz. of recommended daily water intake).

…And a few more tips:

- Sometimes a glass of milk of cup of yogurt really helps take the edge off hunger while you are cooking.

- Try to add a garden salad for lunch and/or dinner or a piece of fruit for breakfast whenever possible.

Here's to your heart health!

Consult your physician before starting any diet or exercise plan, especially if you have medical conditions such as diabetes, hypertension, or any other medical condition or medication that would be affected by diet, exercise or weight loss.